MW00995433

IN THE GROOVE

78
ONLY
"His Master's Voice"

IN THE GROOVE

THE VINYL RECORD AND TURNTABLE REVOLUTION

MATT ANNISS, GILLIAN G. GAAR, KEN MICALLEF,
MARTIN POPOFF & RICHIE UNTERBERGER

Please Please Me – The Beatles
Sgt. Pepper's Lonely Hearts Club Band
AMNESTY INTERNATIONAL PROUDLY PRESENT THE SECRET POLICEMAN'S OTHER BALL THE MUSIC
A&M AMLM 63703
℗ 1975
MARIANNE FAITHFULL
M*A*S*H
ORIGINAL SOUNDTRACK
Love Story – Music From The Original Soundtrack
SLADE THE AMAZING KAMIKAZE SYNDROME
NON-STOP EROTIC CABARET
SLADE ON STAGE
Orchestral Manoeuvres In The Dark
MIKE OLDFIELD
BELLAPHON RECORDS
THE BEST OF GALLAGHER & LYLE
LINDISFARNE / DINGLY DELL
LINDISFARNE / HAPPY DAZE
LINDISFARNE MAGIC IN THE AIR
ONE OF THOSE DAYS IN ENGLAND • (BULLINAMINGVASE)
CARLY SIMON BOYS IN THE TREES
THICK AS A BRICK
JETHRO TULL • MINSTREL IN THE GALLERY
ROLLING STONES RECORDS COC 59106
ROLLING STONES "STILL LIFE" (AMERICAN CONCERT 1981)
SOME GIRLS
A Hard Day's Night – The Beatles
OCTOBERON
SAD CAFE
I'LL TAKE YOU WHERE THE MUSIC'S PLAYING
MIKE HART – MIKE HART BLEEDS
GONG

CONTENTS

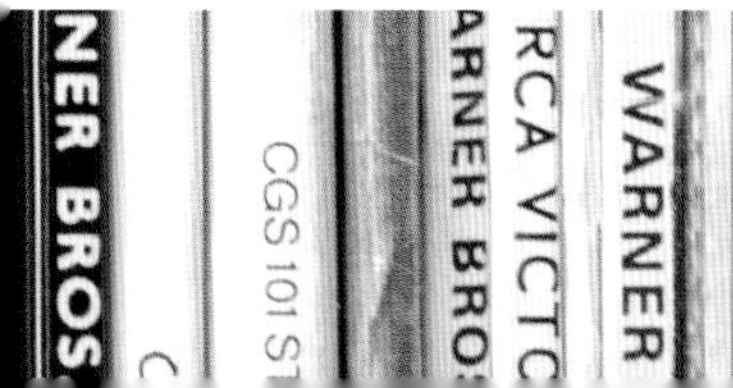

CHAPTER 1

THE BIRTH OF COOL

THE RISE OF THE LP (AND OTHER VINYL FORMATS)

BY RICHIE UNTERBERGER

↑ Of the many music formats that have come and often gone since the late nineteenth century, the 12-inch LP is the most beloved.

The 12-inch vinyl LP was the most popular format for recorded music for only about a quarter century. Yet of the many formats that have come and often gone since the late nineteenth century, the 12-inch LP is the most beloved. For many listeners, its combination of sound quality and artwork can't be beat, even if compact discs, smaller vinyl discs, and electronic files have sometimes been more popular.

THE ROOTS OF THE 12-INCH LP

Although the 12-inch LP didn't start to catch on until the late 1940s, its roots go back to the beginning of the recording industry. Even before records were available for purchase, different formats competed for supremacy as different inventors and manufacturers developed devices for reproducing sound. Thomas Edison's early phonograph played music on wax cylinders, which remained in production more than a decade into the early twentieth century.

But even before the 1880s were out, Emile Berliner came up with a player that used 5-inch flat discs, which had obvious advantages in portability and taking up less storage space. In 1903 the Gramophone Company started offering 12-inch discs, in part because they could play almost twice as long as cylinders. By the end of the first decade of the twentieth century, cylinders were clearly losing out to discs and were completely phased out by the early 1910s.

Why 12 inches? It's not entirely clear, but it might have simply come down to companies from English-speaking countries, particularly the United States, taking the lead in phonograph technology, manufacturing, and distribution.

↑ Thomas Edison's early phonograph played music on wax cylinders, which remained in production more than a decade into the early twentieth century.

← [left] In the 1880s Emile Berliner came up with a player that used 5-inch flat discs, which had obvious advantages in portability and storage.

← [right] The record room at the Berliner Gramophone Company, Montreal, 1910.

Measuring exactly one foot, the 12-inch size was a convenient standard.

However, it was never the only disc diameter on the market. Ten-inch discs also appeared early in the recording industry's history and were the more popular format until the 1950s, its size chosen perhaps simply because it was a round number. Had the early recording market been dominated by countries that used the metric system, it seems quite possible that 30 centimeters (about 11.8 inches) or 25 centimeters (9.84 inches) would have become the standards.

Early 12-inch discs, however, didn't come close to approximating what they'd offer by the middle of the twentieth century. Although they could accommodate more sound, they still had a playing time of just three and a half minutes—a big improvement over the cylinder's mere two minutes but hardly enough to squeeze in full-length operas. The Neophone Company of London tried a 20-inch disc back in 1904 to boost running time, but it suffered from noisy fidelity (even by 1904 standards) and the scarcity of oversize turntables necessary to spin the platter. Edison developed a 12-inch 80rpm (revolutions per minute) disc that could fit up to twenty minutes a side in the mid-1920s, but this also failed due to poor sound and the high cost of the equipment needed to play it.

It would also take quite a while for the 12-inch to standardize its playing speed at 33⅓rpm or even be primarily made of vinyl. Oddly some of the initial impetus came not from the burgeoning music business but the film industry. The Vitaphone record, which synchronized sound and image in early talkies, used a speed of 33⅓ to fit eleven minutes of sound per side. These were actually 16 inches (except for short films) and were obsolete

within a few years as film soundtrack technology rapidly improved. But if the Vitaphone was quickly gone, the speed of 33⅓ was here to stay and was usually, though not always, employed for 12-inch discs within a couple decades.

A couple of technical explanations have been offered for why 33⅓ survived: one to do with gearing reduction ratios, another to how it could get locked into a frequency of 60 hertz per second. The theory that it's simply the subtraction of the popular speed for 7-inch discs (45rpm) from the near-obsolete one the 45 replaced (78rpm) neither seems to be the case nor precisely add up, not accounting for the extra ⅓rpm. In any case, it's an easy value to remember, amounting to exactly one-third of 100rpm.

← [left page] Ten-inch discs also appeared early in the recording industry's history and were the more popular format until the 1950s.

↑ [above] A Gramophone needle on shellac disc. The first commercial discs spinning at 33⅓rpm were released in 1931 but were discontinued within a couple years due to substandard sound quality and the cost of the hardware for playing them.

← [right page] An early audiophile sorts through a pile of 78rpm shellac discs in 1933.

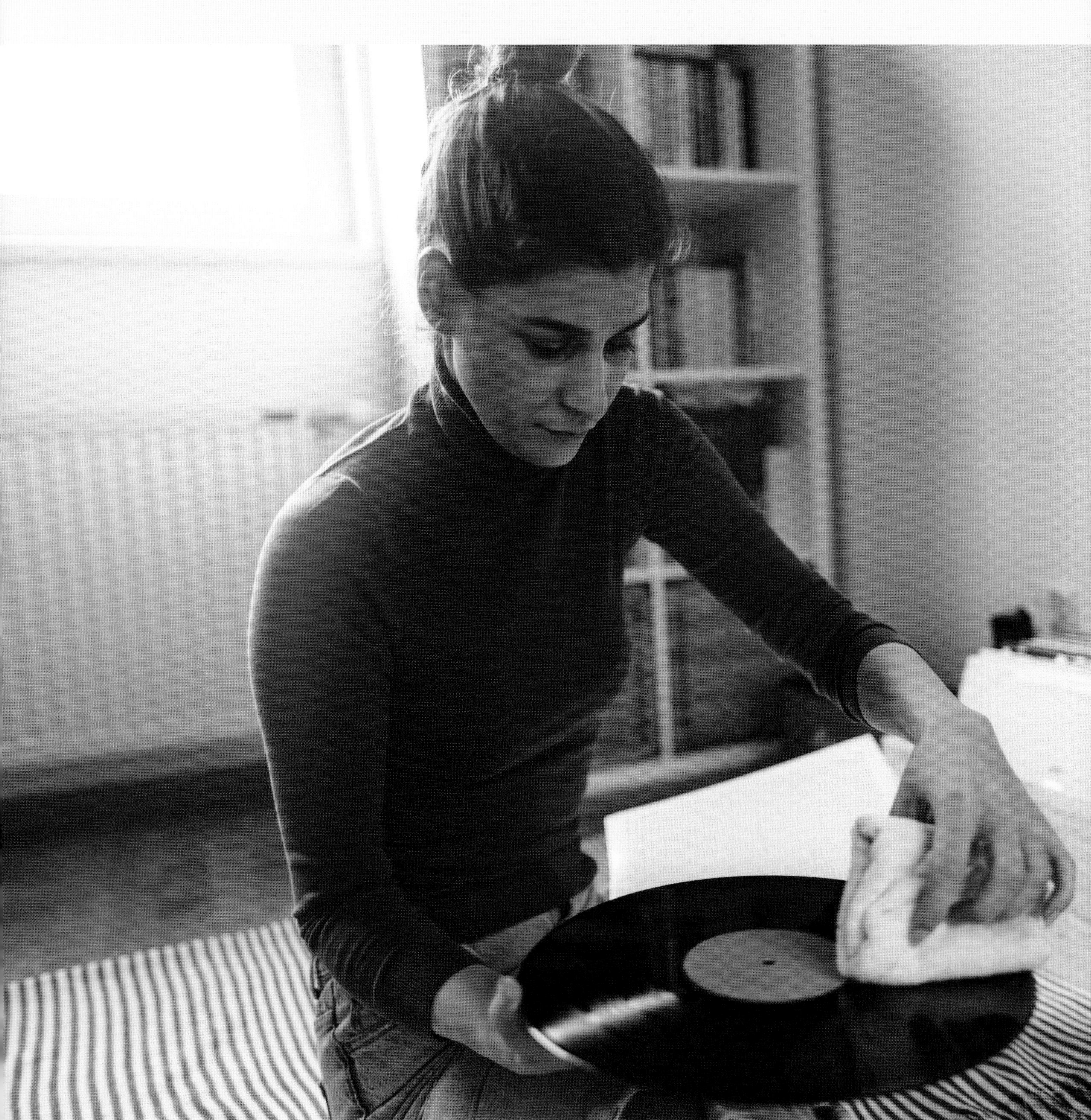

REMARKABLE **RECORD STORES**

TOWER RECORDS

LOS ANGELES, CALIFORNIA

The best-known branch of the iconic Tower chain was located at the intersection of Sunset Boulevard and Horn Avenue. It opened in 1971 and quickly became a mandatory stop for touring musicians. Elton John's visits, when he'd stock up on hundreds of records, became legendary. Music fans were also drawn by the late hours (midnight during the week, 1 a.m. on weekends) and its location near numerous rock clubs. The store closed in 2006. Tower's story is told in the documentary *All Things Must Pass*. –G.G.

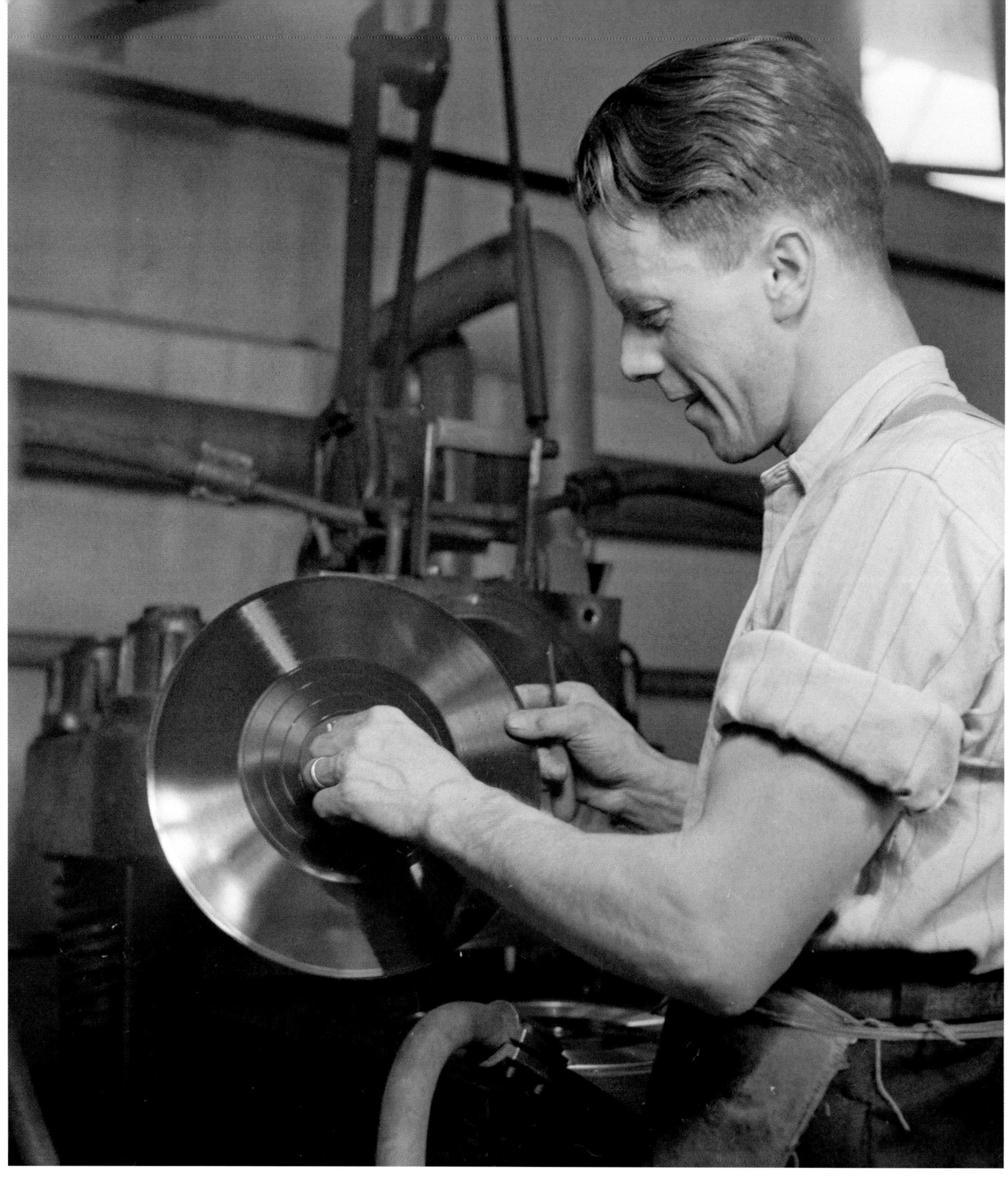

↑ An employee at a Zürich record plant examines a newly pressed record in March 1943. Even before World War II, a new concept in disc packaging addressed a growing hunger to hear more music than a shellac 78 could offer.

THE SHELLAC ERA AND THE BIRTH OF THE "ALBUM"

The first commercial 12-inch (and 10-inch) discs spinning at 33⅓ were released by RCA Victor on November 17, 1931. But they were discontinued within a couple years owing both to substandard sound quality and the cost of the equipment—the "hardware," in today's lingo—for playing them. From World War I to World War II, shellac 78rpm discs would be the norm, dominating the record trade until World War II.

While shellac 78s now might seem like exotic, brittle, and impractical antiquities, there were sound reasons for their prewar prevalence. One had to do with the sound—78s could fit wider grooves than slower speeds, and the fidelity was appreciably better. Another was the ready availability of the raw materials needed to manufacture lots of them as the record industry grew, though that growth was seriously curtailed for nearly a decade by the Depression. That would change with World War II, when other social and scientific upheavals would result in a near-total shift in the size, speed, and substance of most records within a half-decade of war's end.

Even before the war, a new concept in disc packaging addressed a growing hunger to hear more music at once than the mere three minutes and change (about seven if you count both sides of a disc) a shellac 78 could offer. If you wanted to hear the entirety, or at least large chunks, of classical works and operas, or more than seven minutes of your favorite singer or jazz combo, wouldn't you want to buy a bunch of discs in a set instead of buying one at a time here and there?

So, the "album"—a concept not entirely synonymous with the LP, although the terms are sometimes used pretty interchangeably—was born. Record albums date back as far as 1910, if they're thought of in the same way as photo albums, binding together empty sleeves into which discs could be slotted. Strangely it wasn't until the 1930s that labels took what in retrospect seems to be the next logical step: issuing collections of several 78s featuring a single performer, style, or symphony. The way such tracks would be grouped together would change radically over the next few years, yet the term *album* has stuck, even now that some "albums" don't even have a physical form.

By the 1940s there were albums boasting multiple discs by the likes of Ella Fitzgerald, Louis Armstrong, Lionel Hampton, and Paul Robeson. The next obvious—if, again, at least in hindsight—step was to dress up the packaging with specially designed cover artwork, starting with a 1940 album of four 78s titled *Smash Song Hits by Rodgers & Hart*. This was designed by Alex Steinweiss, whose 1942 cover for Beethoven's *Piano Concerto no. 5 in E-flat* had a rainbow-like line of colors like the one seen on Pink Floyd's *The Dark Side of the Moon*, though it's doubtful the designers of the 1973 megasmash had seen it.

While the demand for such albums, and for recorded music in general, might have been growing as the world rebounded from the Depression, the war almost ground the music business to a halt in the early 1940s. Shellac was produced by beetle secretions, mostly in the Malay Peninsula and French Indochina; when Japanese forces occupied the territories, the supply dried up. What's more, citizens were encouraged to turn in their shellac discs so they could be recycled for wartime production. This likely contributed to the rarity or even outright loss of some historically important recordings that only existed in that format, such as some early blues 78s (like two of the three cut by Willie Brown in 1930) known to have been issued but never rediscovered.

On top of this, an American Federation of Musicians (AFM) strike in mid-1942 all but canceled the production of newly recorded discs until late 1944. On the surface, these seemed like near-death blows to an industry perched on the verge of a boom. Yet they also directly led to innovations that would fuel the growth of the 12-inch vinyl disc and help catapult the record business into unprecedented growth within just a decade.

To both boost military morale and offer musicians at least some outlet during the AFM strike, V-Discs—named both for "Victory" and a key force behind their production, sound engineer G. Robert

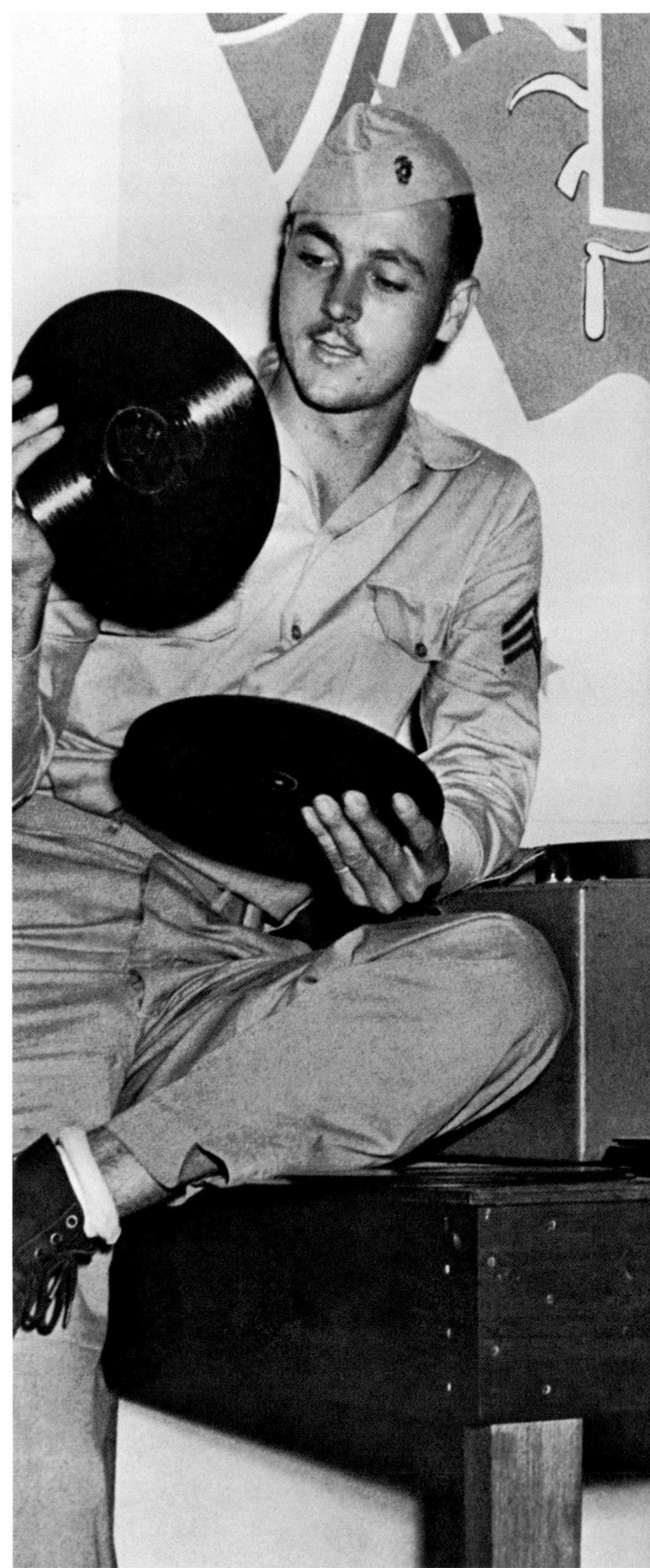

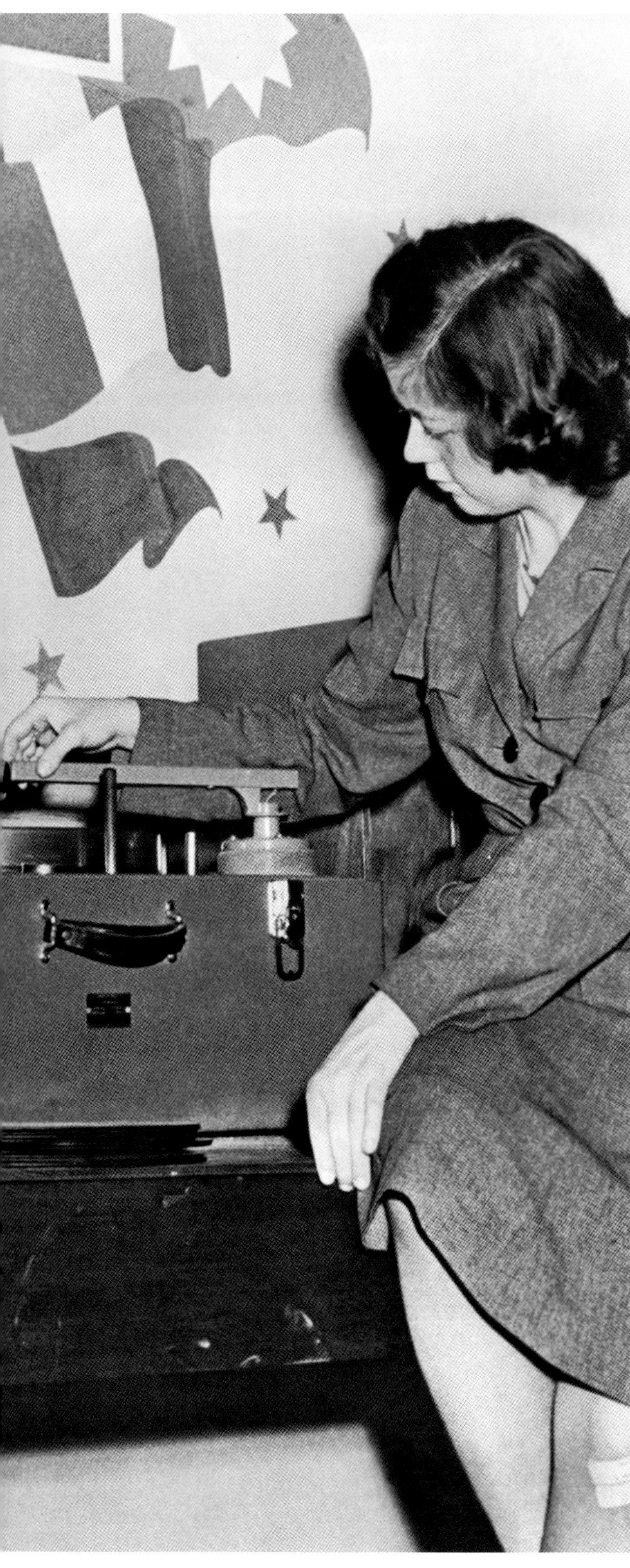

← A U.S. Marine Corps sergeant and a Red Cross staffer pick out records in the game room of a service club. Created to help boost allied morale in World War II, V-Discs could hold six minutes per side and were a substantial improvement on shellac 78s. And they measured 12 inches and were made from vinyl—the standards adopted for the long-playing records already in development.

Vincent—were cut by stars like Frank Sinatra and Duke Ellington. They could hold six minutes per side, not nearly as long as LPs that would appear by the end of the 1940s, and were a substantial improvement on shellac 78s. And they measured 12 inches and were made from vinyl—the standards adopted for the long-playing records already in development (though it would take a few years before they'd be available to the public).

V-Discs went out of production in 1949, and not many survive today, in part because they (and the masters from which they were made) were supposed to have been destroyed after they'd performed their official function of supplying entertainment for troops. Naturally a few escaped demolition, whether hoarded by collectors or overlooked in the order to wipe out their existence. By the time they ceased production, however, they were being rapidly superseded by long-playing records that contained much more music and, of more importance, were available to anyone who wanted to buy them.

BLEECKER BOB'S RECORDS
BLEECKER BOB'S
HOLLYWOOD
ATM
Since 1956

REMARKABLE **RECORD STORES**

BLEECKER BOB'S RECORDS

NEW YORK, NEW YORK

In 1967 Robert Plotnik and Al Trommers opened Village Oldies in Greenwich Village, specializing in blues, doo-wop, and R&B. The shop eventually took on Trommers's nickname for Plotnik and broadened its music stock, becoming a home base for the Big Apple's nascent punk scene (and an occasional employer of those in the scene, including Lenny Kaye). Bleecker Bob's was name-checked in a Beastie Boys song and featured in a *Seinfeld* episode. The store moved to different locations around the Village before finally closing in 2013. –*G.G.*

THE BIRTH OF THE VINYL LP

By the mid-1940s, Columbia Records, one of the most powerful major record labels, had undertaken serious research and development into the creation of a long-playing record—or LP, the abbreviation that's been in common use ever since—that could fit far more music, with better sound quality, than any previous discs. By 1947, using vinyl that could fit 224–300 microgrooves per inch, they'd devised LPs that could run for 22½ minutes per side.

These were introduced to the world at a June 18, 1948, press conference in New York's Waldorf Astoria Hotel. More than 100 Columbia LPs—mostly classical, as well as some pop and children's discs—were soon on the market, though these were 10-inch platters. Now that music could be recorded on tape, it was also possible for LPs to boast sound quality that was a vast improvement over any discs predating the 1940s.

Perhaps embarrassed and indignant at being scooped by a chief competitor, RCA soon countered with a vinyl 7-inch format (technically measuring 6⅞ inches) in hopes of capturing listeners with shorter attention spans and smaller budgets. (RCA tried a 6-inch 40rpm format before going with 7 inches and 45rpm.)

But the LP was here to stay, with powerhouse record companies Capitol and Decca both starting to issue long-players in 1949. RCA joined the LP brigade in early 1950. Both the LP and the single—or 45, as it would also be termed, in honor of its usual 45rpm speed—would become hugely popular formats over the next few decades, even if their appeal would vary widely and sometimes target very different listeners.

Although LPs and singles would never exclusively be made from vinyl, the substance was so commonly used for records that the term *vinyl* and the discs you play with a stylus became virtually synonymous. Why vinyl, and why did it take so relatively long to become industry standard?

Vinyl—short for polyvinyl chloride or PVC—was first produced in the early 1930s and almost immediately was used in radio program transcriptions. Because it was more expensive to manufacture than shellac, however, it took World War II to force its wider use, especially on the 8 million or so V-Discs.

45 MINUTES OF MUSIC FROM A SINGLE RECORD

. . . ANOTHER "FIRST" BY COLUMBIA RECORDS

Finer tone quality! So lifelike you'll hardly believe you're listening to a record. Low notes, high notes are heard without distortion. And practically no surface noise!

Uninterrupted music! Major works are recorded either on 2 sides or 1 side of a single LP record. At last—no more annoying "breaks."

More than twice as much music for your money! Columbia LP Records save you up to 60% per selection over conventional Vinylite records. Think how much farther your music budget goes . . . how much faster you'll build a fine record collection.

Nonbreakable Vinylite! Makes broken records practically a thing of the past—another source of savings. And super-smooth Vinylite means finer tone.

Saves storage space! Every inch of shelf space holds 3 hours of music!

Over 600 selections already in catalog! Symphonies, concertos, musical comedies, jazz, opera, children's stories —157 different records! A wonderful collection of entertainment by your favorite artists who record exclusively for Columbia. Many new releases every month.

THIS COLUMBIA (Lp) PLAYER ATTACHMENT

plays LP records through your present radio or phonograph

You only need to add a slow-speed player attachment to your present set in order to play LP Records. The handsome Columbia Player shown here is quickly installed, attractively priced, and precision-designed for flawless reproduction of Columbia LP Records. It modernizes your present set to play *both* LP and your regular records. Has amazing featherweight tone arm weighing only ⅕ of an ounce! Your savings on a few LP Records pay for it.

See your dealer today!

"Columbia," "Masterworks" and ®® Trade Marks Reg. U. S. Pat. Off. Marcas Registradas ® Trade Mark

↑ Two turntables and a microphone. Composer and bandleader Duke Ellington holds records in each hand as he stands over a radio DJ's desk during an appearance in the late 1940s.

While RCA started to use the more durable vinyl for some classical releases in 1946, it took the introduction of LPs to make its use common.

The overwhelming majority of vinyl releases of all kinds would be black, but it's actually not the substance's natural color. The reason it's usually black is sensibly prosaic: It's the color that makes it easiest to distinguish the separate tracks and place the needle, particularly for radio DJs (and later club DJs).

ICONIC **COVERS**

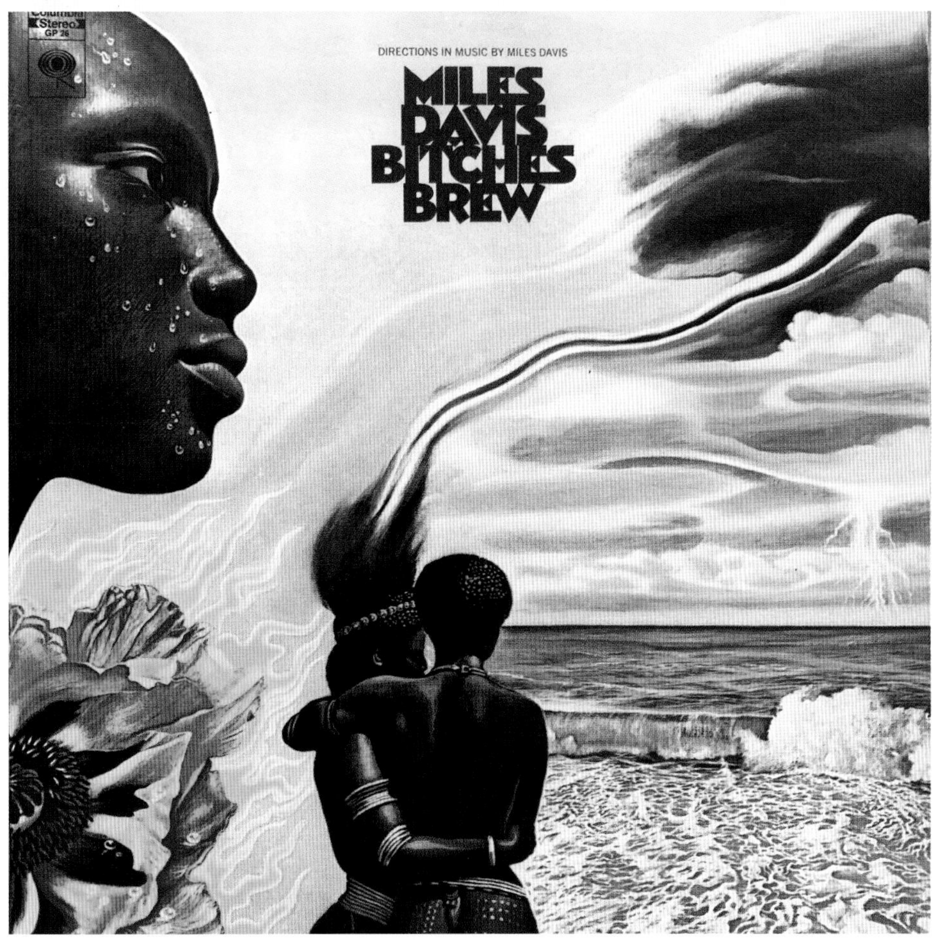

BITCHES BREW • MILES DAVIS

This action-packed cover art for a challenging double album was created by French surrealist painter Malti Klarwein, a sort of Black culture psychedelia, with a statement about how humankind is also part of climate and nature. It's bold and dramatic and almost paranormal, raising expectations for the music enclosed, as does the additional movie poster–styled text that reads, "Directions in Music by Miles Davis." *–M.P.*

THE RISE OF THE 45RPM SINGLE

Postwar shifts in social and musical tastes ensured that 7-inch discs—usually, though not always, featuring just one song on each side—were more popular than LPs for quite some time.

One factor was the exploding market for what today might be considered "roots" music but back in the late 1940s was often referred to as "race" or "hillbilly." The "race" discs were aimed primarily at African Americans, including many who were migrating from the rural South to urban areas; "hillbilly" records targeted whites of modest means, often in the South. Music trade publications modified these labels to the more dignified "rhythm and blues" (R&B) and "country and western," and these audiences often preferred discs spotlighting just one song, filled out with a flip side or "B-side." As it happens, the first R&B 45, released by RCA in March 1949, was a historically important one: Arthur Crudup's "That's All Right, Mama" (first issued on 78 in 1947), which Elvis Presley would cover in mid-1954 on his first single.

Country and R&B fans wanted the jolt of a particularly juicy song or two at once and sometimes lacked the cash to splurge for much more expensive LPs. Sometimes they didn't even have the equipment to play records, helping to spur a jukebox industry so huge that *Billboard* had a jukebox chart from 1940 to 1957, with about three-quarters of U.S. records going into jukeboxes rather than homes in the mid-1940s. Jukebox operators much preferred 7-inch discs to LPs, ensuring quick turnover as patrons fed coins into the machines. They also preferred 7-inch discs to shellac 10-inch discs, since jukeboxes could hold more discs of that size.

Vinyl's greater durability also made them far preferable to shellac, especially in jukeboxes where singles would get far more plays than they would in homes. DJs at the burgeoning numbers of radio stations and programs playing blues and country also

→ A man peers at a spinning 7-inch record inside a Rock-Ola jukebox, circa 1955. Jukebox operators much preferred 7-inch discs to LPs, ensuring quick turnover as patrons fed coins into the machines.

OCK·OLA
RECORD PLAYING

REMARKABLE **RECORD STORES**

JAZZ RECORD MART • *CHICAGO, ILLINOIS*

Bob Koester opened what he liked to call "the world's largest jazz and blues record store" in the late 1950s, giving it the name Jazz Record Mart in 1962. While jazz fans from around the world searched through the bins, aspiring musicians who worked in the store, such as trumpeter Josh Berman, would be rehearsing in the back room. The store closed in 2016, when Koester sold the stock to Wolfgang's Vault, which buys and sells music-related items. –G.G.

wanted singles, which were much easier to cue up and quickly segue between than LP tracks. They were also far more suited toward playing over and over as single-song "hits" that listeners demanded and which stations kept in constant rotation to build audiences and advertising.

It wasn't a given that all singles would be 7 inches and spin at 45rpm. The 78 remained in production in the United States throughout the 1950s, and in the earlier part of the decade, many singles (including Presley's early releases) were available on both 45 and 78. But by the mid-1950s, when the fusion of country and R&B led to the rock 'n' roll explosion, 45rpm was clearly winning out, with customers and businesspeople alike finding them lighter, easier to store, and less apt to get damaged than 78s. Teenagers played a big part in this victory, since they were a huge part of rock 'n' roll's demographic and more apt to buy singles than albums owing to income limitations. The industry had to

↓ Seven-inch discs—usually, though not always, featuring just one song on each side—were more popular than LPs for quite some time.

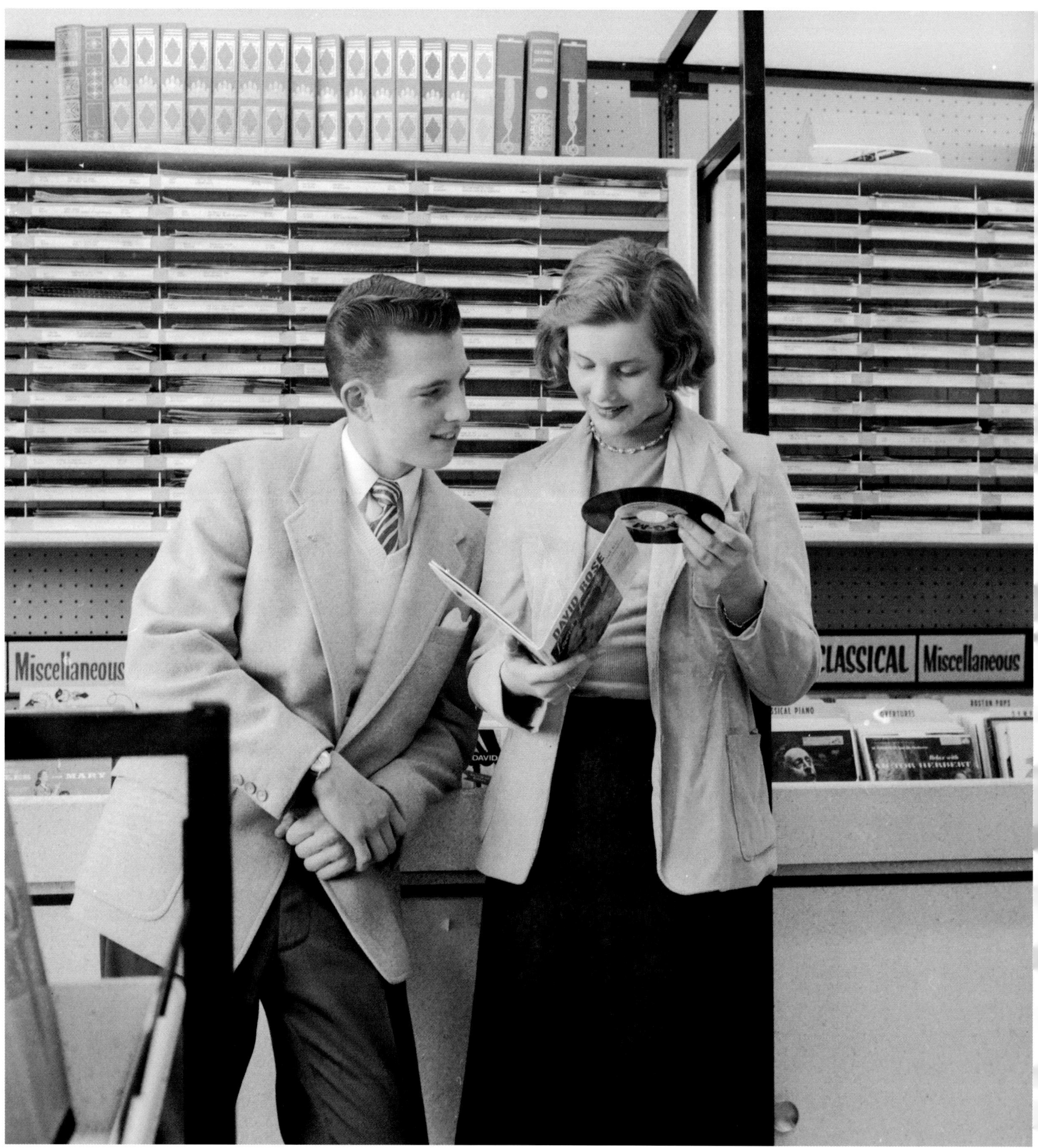
Miscellaneous
CLASSICAL
Miscellaneous
DAVID ROSE

put their production of 45s into overdrive as the demand for discs grew beyond anyone's expectations, with record sales more than tripling between 1950 ($189 million) and 1960 ($603 million).

Some purists maintain that 78s offer better fidelity with the right equipment. As Charlie Gillett wrote in his seminal history *The Sound of the City: The Rise of Rock and Roll*, "Played through the huge speakers of jukeboxes, 78s delivered a massive sound which can only be vaguely approximated by CDs on a domestic hi-fi or portable system. Owners of Elvis's 78rpm singles on Sun justifiably believe that no other format has come close to reproducing their impact." Jim Dawson, coauthor of *What Was the First Rock 'n' Roll Record?* and *45 RPM*, agrees, telling National Public Radio's *The Record* that 78s "could accommodate wider grooves (great for bass). It was actually one of the best music carriers; far superior to 45s in that regard. Once you hear 1950s R&B and rock 'n' roll on a 78 jukebox, everything else will sound anemic."

Nonetheless 78s were virtually phased out of production in the United States by the beginning of the 1960s, though they hung on longer in some countries, particularly India, which put out Beatles singles on 78 all the way through 1968's "Hey Jude." Many collectors prefer 45rpm versions of singles even if the tracks are easily available on full-length albums, as the deeper grooves on 7-inch discs usually produce markedly louder volume. It's harder to fit that fidelity into the grooves when singles go longer than four or five minutes, but The Beatles were so big by 1968 that EMI put out all seven minutes-plus of "Hey Jude" on one side of a 45.

← Teenagers examine a 45 in a record store around 1956. Seven-inch records were far more suitable for playing hits over and over.

OTHER SPEEDS AND FORMATS

At the other end of the scale, some 16rpm discs of various sizes were introduced in the late 1950s that could hold about twice as many minutes as 33⅓ records. Used mostly for spoken-word recordings, this speed failed to make more than the tiniest dent in record sales, though many record players over the next decade or so had a 16rpm option.

It wasn't even a given that all 7-inch discs would have one A-side and one B-side. B-sides had been on discs since the early twentieth century and standard features on records by the mid-1920s. They were often produced with far more haste and far less care than the side meant to attract radio play and sales, sometimes designated the "plug" side.

However, many B-sides became the A-sides when radio DJs played the "wrong" one. Such classic hits as Bill Haley's "Rock Around the Clock," Cliff Richard's "Move It" (usually regarded as the first great British rock song), and Booker T. & the MG's' "Green Onions" were originally B-sides, among many other examples. When The Beatles and other bands began putting B-sides on their 45s that were as good or almost as good as the A-sides, the distinction almost became meaningless, resulting in double-sided hits like "We Can Work It Out"/"Day Tripper." Long before that, Elvis Presley had a double-sided 1956 chart-topper with "Hound Dog"/"Don't Be Cruel"; and his five 1954–1955 classic Sun Records rockabilly singles each paired a blues-oriented number with a country-oriented selection, broadening their appeal and giving radio stations with different formats wider options.

In addition, the extended-play disc, or EP—usually, but not always, 7 inches in diameter—has been around almost as long as the LP, usually (again, not always) offering about twice as much music as the single. Most often these had four tracks, though sometimes they offered three or five. The idea was to offer a sort of midpoint for fans who wanted more than two songs but didn't want to pay for more expensive LPs. Sometimes EPs sort of sold an LP's worth of material on an installment plan, though EPs have also been used to showcase material not available on other formats.

The EP was never as popular in the United States as the 7-inch single or LP but more popular in the 1950s than many realize. Many early rock 'n' roll stars—including Elvis, Little Richard, and Ricky Nelson—put out EPs, whose sales were considered significant enough to merit a separate *Billboard* chart from 1957 to 1960. In the United Kingdom and some other countries, EPs

ICONIC **COVERS**

SGT. PEPPER'S LONEY HEARTS CLUB BAND • THE BEATLES

The original idea by Peter Blake and Jann Haworth was of The Beatles standing for a picture with members of a crowd that had just seen the band perform. This morphed into the idea that it could be an idealized crowd of famous people, accomplished through the use of cardboard cutouts, which lent a psychedelic paste-up feel to the proceedings. Also sending it psych was the portrayal of the band dressed in an explosion of color, each with a moustache (but not particularly long hair). –M.P.

LEGENDARY **LABELS**

SUN RECORDS

The Memphis label is most known for issuing Elvis Presley's first five singles in 1954–1955 before selling his contract to RCA for a then-massive sum of $35,000. It was arguably the most influential independent label in setting rock 'n' roll in motion with Elvis and rockabilly hits by Carl Perkins, Johnny Cash, and Jerry Lee Lewis. Before that, Sun cut great blues sides by Junior Parker, Rufus Thomas, Little Milton, James Cotton, and others. But it was the combination of R&B and country music, overseen by Sam Phillips, that was crucial to the birth of rock 'n' roll, cementing Sun's place in the history books. The distinctive Sun logo, with a rooster crowing amid a burst of yellow rays, is among the most coveted by collectors; and Presley's original Sun 78s are among the priciest rarities in good condition. –R.U.

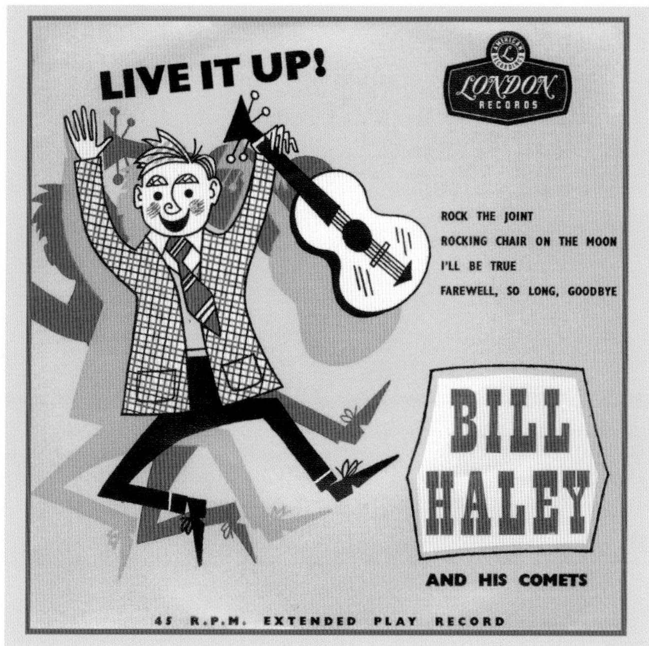

LIVE IT UP!
LONDON
RECORDS
ROCK THE JOINT
ROCKING CHAIR ON THE MOON
I'LL BE TRUE
FAREWELL, SO LONG, GOODBYE
BILL
HALEY
AND HIS COMETS
45 R.P.M. EXTENDED PLAY RECORD

← The extended-play disc, or EP, most often has four tracks, though sometimes they offer three or five. Originally the idea was to offer a sort of midpoint for fans who wanted more than two songs but didn't want to pay for more expensive LPs.

were more common and accounted for a far higher percentage of sales, owing both to less disposable income for British teenagers and simple preferences in some territories for the format. In France, for instance, the EP was the primary format for 7-inch discs until the late 1960s, the country issuing more Beatles EPs than Beatles singles before 1967.

EPs by British rock stars were common through the mid-1960s, though they were almost entirely discontinued in the United Kingdom by the end of the decade. Yet they made an unexpected comeback in the punk and new wave era, with artists and independent labels seizing an opportunity to put out intermediate sorts of releases if they had more than two songs but not enough for an LP.

There was even a revival of different-sized formats: The Clash's *Black Market Clash* compiling B-sides and other rarities onto one 10-inch EP, for example. In keeping with the punk spirit, some releases subverted long-accepted standards of vinyl production. Japanese pop-punkers Shonen Knife releasing an 8-inch (20 cm) EP. Arty Italian ensemble Degenerazione Musicale drilled holes in the grooves between the tracks of a late-1980s EP, and listeners had to lift the needle between every song to make sure the needle didn't get stuck and possibly damaged.

EXTENDED PLAY

NOTABLE EPS

While EPs often merely grouped together a couple singles or an assortment of tracks available on 45s and LPs, some presented unique content otherwise unavailable at the time of their release, especially in the United Kingdom. Some of the most notable examples include the following:

→ **The Beatles, *Long Tall Sally*** (Parlophone, United Kingdom, June 1964). Their tremendous cover of Little Richard's hit titles this four-song platter, also featuring cool versions of Larry Williams's "Slow Down" and Carl Perkins's "Matchbox," as well as the Lennon-McCartney original "I Call Your Name." Technically, "Long Tall Sally" and "I Call Your Name" had already been released in the United States a couple months earlier on *The Beatles Second Album*, but few British fans would have been able to buy that in 1964.

→ **The Rolling Stones, *5 × 5*** (Decca, United Kingdom, August 1964). Prime early Stones with one of their best Chuck Berry covers ("Around and Around"), the great group-written instrumental "2120 South Michigan Avenue," a decent early original in "Empty Heart," and good covers of soul (Wilson Pickett's "If You Need Me") and blues ("Confessin' the Blues"). All five of the songs were on the Stones' second U.S. LP, which expanded the title to *12 × 5*, a couple months later.

→ **Country Joe & the Fish, *Country Joe & the Fish*** (Rag Baby, United States, July 1966). Some of the earliest and best Bay Area psychedelic rock was on this three-song EP, particularly the fabulous instrumental "Section 43." All three of the songs were redone for their first album, but "Section 43" in particular is looser and better here. This was conveniently combined with EP-only releases by other 1960s Bay Area bands of the time (Mad River, Frumious Bandersnatch, and Notes from the Underground) for the 1995 CD compilation *The Berkeley EPs.*

→ **The Who, *Ready Steady Who*** (Reaction, United Kingdom, November 1966). The title led some to believe this was live because it referenced the great British pop music TV program *Ready Steady Go.* But these were studio tracks, including a couple decent Pete Townshend originals ("Circles" in a different version from the U.S. *My Generation* album and "Disguises"), and a bunch of off-the-wall covers ("Batman," Jan & Dean's "Bucket T," and "Barbara Ann"). "Disguises" and "Bucket T" came out on the U.S. *Magic Bus* album in 1968, but the other tracks weren't released Stateside until many years later. *–R.U.*

THE RISE AND HEYDAY OF THE LP

While the LP faced some stiff competition from singles and (to a far lesser degree) from EPs for its first two decades, it was never in danger of extinction. The increased availability and growing sophistication of home record players played a part, as did marketing that targeted a more affluent and adult audience than the younger fans of the rock 'n' roll dominating the singles charts from the mid-1950s onward. Generally the early LP market prioritized classical works, soundtracks, theatrical musicals, and mainstream popular crooners like Frank Sinatra, as well as jazz and folk long-players that would often be released on independent labels targeting specialized niche audiences.

More and more artists became equally or more popular through LPs than singles, including Sinatra, who was one of the first stars to aim for establishing definite moods and themes through a long-player; Harry Belafonte, whose calypso albums sold massive quantities that spanned ethnicities and generations; and folkies The Kingston Trio, who at one point had four LPs in the Top Ten. The LP was also far more suited for presenting long comedy routines that would have been impossible to fit on singles, whether from daring cutting-edgers like Lenny Bruce and Dick Gregory, comics like Moms Mabley targeting a black audience, or bestsellers like Bob Newhart.

Both 10- and 12-inch LPs were common through around the mid-1950s. But much as 45s won out over 78s, the 12-inch LP was the clear victor by the end of the decade, likely because it was apt to hold more music and bigger, better artwork. Most LPs would run between thirty and forty-five minutes, as sound quality risked compromise at longer playing times. There would be exceptions, ranging from the U.K. version of The Rolling Stones' 1966 LP *Aftermath* (fifty-three minutes) and Todd Rundgren's 1975 effort *Initiation* (sixty-eight minutes) to the Pye label's *Golden Hour*series and Barry Manilow's *The Manilow Collection: 20 Classic Hits*, which had a whopping seventy-five minutes.

→ **The LP was also far more suited for presenting long comedy routines that would have been impossible to fit on singles, thus opening new audiences for cutting-edgers like Lenny Bruce.**

THE SICK HUMOR
of LENNY BRUCE
Fantasy
7003
HIGH FIDELITY

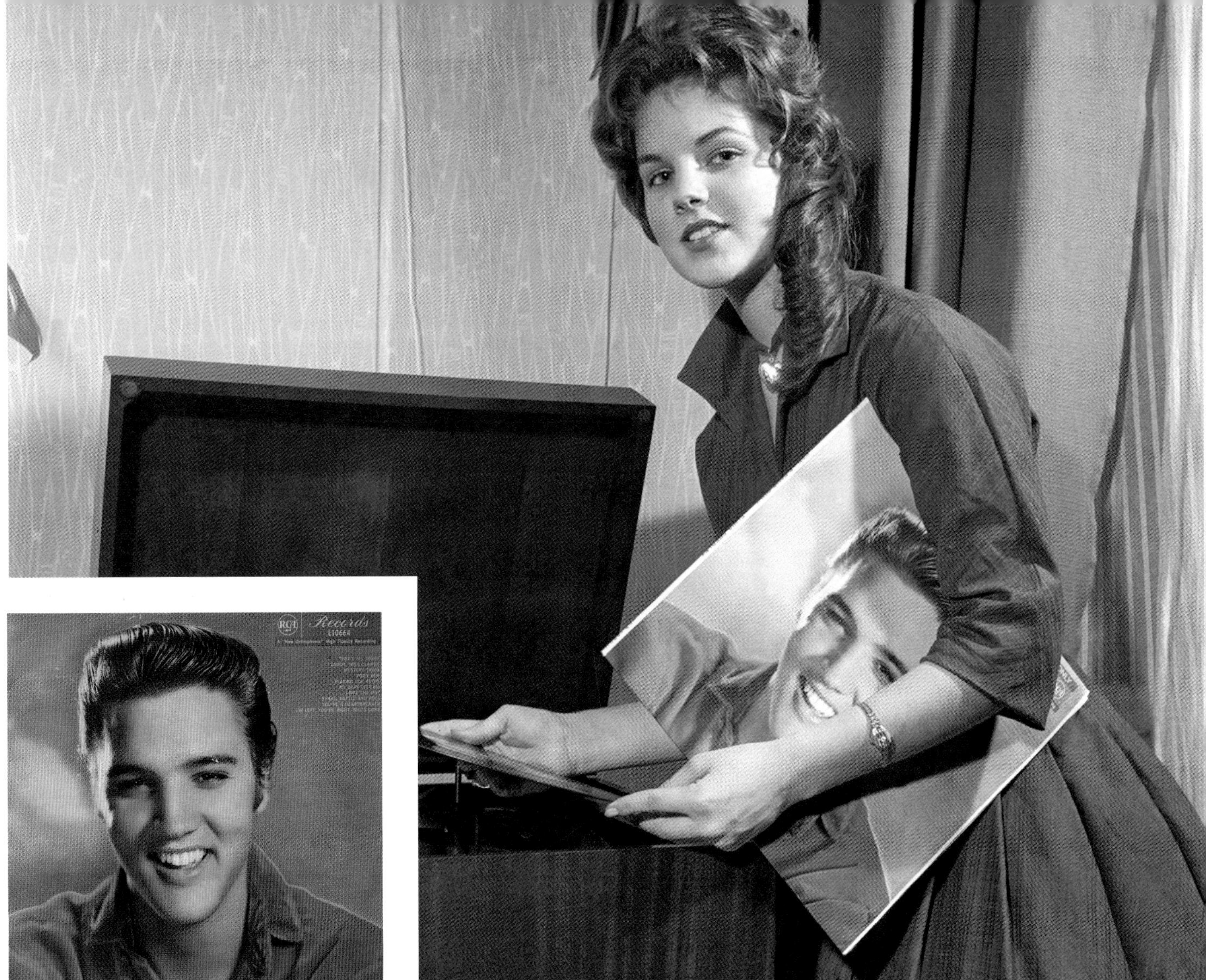

↑ Young Priscilla Beaulieu plays an LP record by a certain teen idol who was serving in the U.S. Army in Germany at the time. Early rock 'n' roll stars weren't absent from the new LP chart. Presley sold huge numbers of albums.

Rock 'n' roll stars weren't absent from the new LP chart. Presley, in particular, sold huge numbers of albums; and virtually every rock 'n' roller of the 1950s and early 1960s who had a few hits (and many who didn't) had at least one LP. But the expanding rock and soul industry paid far greater attention to singles than albums, often padding out one or two hits with lower-quality filler.

There were exceptions. Some of Elvis's albums were excellent, as were some by the Everly Brothers and Buddy Holly that clearly paid far more attention to consistently fine material than LPs by most of their peers. Even before he had big pop hits, James Brown demonstrated that an exciting live

ICONIC **COVERS**

LED ZEPPELIN • LED ZEPPELIN

Pretty much every Led Zeppelin album cover is hall aflame material, but we've picked the first one because the image itself is iconic, namely an ink rendering by George Hardie of Sam Shere's photograph depicting the Hindenburg on fire. There's added significance because Hardie would go on to do more famed work for Zeppelin and others, along with the fact that the artful back cover shot is by The Yardbirds' Chris Dreja, who would go on to a respected career as a photographer. *–M.P.*

LEGENDARY **LABELS**

FOLKWAYS

Folkways was one of the first labels to embrace the LP as a vehicle for highly specialized music appealing to a niche market rather than the general pop audience. As its name announced, it specialized in folk music, recording all sorts of genres with traditional roots from the United States and around the world. At a time when many folk performers had their livelihoods threatened by McCarthy-era blacklisting, Folkways chief Moe Asch gave performers like Pete Seeger and Woody Guthrie a chance to keep recording and releasing material. The plainly designed Folkways albums were never going to win awards for packaging, but the label was vital to helping launch the folk revival, its catalog eventually bulging to more than 2,000 LPs (and even venturing into rock with The Fugs' debut long-player). Much of its catalog has been reissued on CD by Smithsonian Folkways. *–R.U.*

album could scale the charts, with his *Live at the Apollo* peaking at #2 in 1963. But it wasn't until the mid-1960s, when artists like The Beatles who treated the album as an art form burst on the scene, that the rock LP began to rival the rock single in popularity.

The introduction of stereo records in the late 1950s was also key in maintaining and even expanding the audience for LPs. The first stereo discs were issued by Audio Fidelity in March 1958, one geared toward showing off a range of sound effects (*Railroad: The Sounds of a Vanishing Era*), another featuring an established jazz star, Lionel Hampton. Many early stereo LPs were sort of gimmicky devices for demonstrating the new two-channel format, particularly sound effects records and the sort of oddball lounge jazz that would later be labeled "exotica" or even "space age bachelor pad music."

But stereo quickly caught on in all formats, even if its appeal was somewhat limited in its early years to those who could afford the considerably more expensive equipment needed to get the most of it. Rock 'n' roll, although by some measures the most popular music in the record business by the 1960s, was not as quick to get on board as might have been expected. With its demographic still dominated by teenagers, it was assumed they'd be less likely to afford stereo equipment—or be allowed to play it often or at all on their parents' stereos.

So, many rock and soul releases continued to be issued in mono; and if they were available in both stereo and mono editions, often considerably less attention was paid to the stereo iteration. This was more pronounced in the United Kingdom, even after the British Invasion had made British rock a huge force in the record business. With a markedly lower average income, young British rock fans were far less likely to have stereo equipment than their American counterparts.

Until the late 1960s, British rock musicians paid far more attention to the mono mixes than stereo; and mono remained the primary U.K. format. Mono editions of Beatles albums, for instance, were available as late as 1968's self-titled LP (a.k.a. the "White Album"). Such was the low esteem in which stereo was sometimes held that gauche "electronically reprocessed for stereo" LPs were concocted for the American market. Even The Beatles and The Rolling Stones were subjected to such treatment, though the process sometimes made the records sound as tinny as transistor radios.

But much as 45s had overtaken 78s and vinyl had overtaken shellac (and, later, how CDs would overtake LPs), by the end of the 1960s, mono was getting phased out. Stereo equipment was becoming not just more common but the

DECCA
AFTER
-MATH
AFTER
-MATH

norm, backed by the mushrooming popularity of FM stereo radio (particularly "underground" FM rock stations).

Albums were, after nearly twenty years, finally surpassing singles in sales, especially as stars like The Beatles, Beach Boys, Bob Dylan, and (if a bit later) soul legends like Stevie Wonder and Marvin Gaye crafted LPs as serious full-length artistic statements. This even extended to the design, with the *Sgt. Pepper's Lonely Hearts Club Band*'s cover becoming about as well known as any twentieth-century artwork, and with esteemed artists like Andy Warhol designing covers for major stars like The Rolling Stones. Designers like the Hipgnosis team responsible for many Pink Floyd covers became stars in their own right, with a 12 × 12-inch canvas that would be seriously hampered with the advent of CDs.

In addition, icons like Jimi Hendrix could become superstars without huge hit singles, and more cultish underground figures like the Mothers of Invention would sustain long careers by selling records through FM radio, word of mouth, and the booming circuit for underground rock concerts. This was more or less confirmed by *Billboard* magazine's August 18, 1967, announcement that "the LP is threatening the single's long-held dominance in the launching of pop artists. Record company executives have discovered that the new type of groups being launched on discs don't need single hits to sell albums."

By mid-1968, albums accounted for more than 75 percent of record sales. And while the multidisc format had previously mostly been reserved for classical albums and non-rock projects, double rock LPs came onto the market by Hendrix, The Beatles, Cream, and other rock stars, with the *Woodstock* soundtrack and George Harrison's *All Things Must Pass* even introducing triple LPs into the equation in 1970.

← Nattily attired young "Mods" hang out in Chelsea, London, in 1966. By 1967, *Billboard* magazine was declaring that "the LP is threatening the single's long-held dominance in the launching of pop artists."

STEREO VS. MONO, AND OTHER VARIATIONS

This period of hectic transition led to a proliferation of LP variants that are among the most hungrily sought by collectors more than half a century later. In the mid- to late-1960s, many classic rock albums (and quite a few not-so-classic ones) were issued in both stereo and mono. Which format is "better" seems very much to depend on the listener, analyst, and specific record. Generally the louder and more straight-ahead rockers are considered better in mono, with the more elaborate and delicate productions better in stereo.

Keep in mind, however, that both stereo and mono are vociferously championed by different enthusiasts and their merits sometimes so hotly debated that a classic album can be deemed both vastly preferable and dismissed as worthless in its stereo (or mono) edition. Sometimes entirely different vocal and instrumental parts are present or missing in different versions; sometimes entirely different takes were used. Although they're much rarer, there are also variants where different stereo editions have noticeably different mixes.

There's another reason why original pressings from the 1960s and 1970s are still coveted, even over remastered for vinyl reissues with twenty-first-century technology. "There is no doubt that, with the occasional exception, you will invariably get better sound on the first or initial pressings of a record, particularly in relation to 1960s and 1970s releases, when the art of cutting vinyl was at its peak," says Alec Palao, who has compiled, annotated, and produced hundreds of reissues for labels like Ace and Rhino. "And a general rule of thumb is that pressings from the country where the artist is from, or where they tended to record, will sound the best. Even countries whose pressings are feted, such as Japan, still had to rely on supplied copy masters as a cutting source when issuing overseas material.

"In the U.K., vintage 7's are often the only way to hear the singles material of the era—for example, the difference between the cut of U.K. and U.S. Beatles singles is marked. A classic like 'Friday on My Mind' by The Easybeats is still best heard from the original U.K. United Artists pressing from late 1966. There are always exceptions—U.S. pressings were always renowned in the U.K. for their prominent bass level. But when I interviewed [Booker T. & the MG's guitarist] Steve Cropper some years ago, he commented that when he first visited the U.K. as part of the Stax/Volt tour in early 1967, he was amazed at the punch

REMARKABLE **RECORD STORES**

AQUARIUS RECORDS • *SAN FRANCISCO, CALIFORNIA*

The 1960s might have been over when Aquarius opened its doors in 1970, but it still carried the torch for the San Francisco sound, having a fine stock of psychedelia and also known for curating an excellent selection of more esoteric fare, such as carrying world music artists before the term had even been coined. Aquarius closed in 2016, then reopened under new ownership as Stranded Records. There's also a documentary, *It Came from Aquarius Records*. –G.G.

ONE CHANNEL OR TWO?

MONO VS. STEREO

The differences between stereo and mono versions of classic 1960s rock tracks could fill up a book for The Beatles alone. Following are just a very few striking instances:

→ **The Beatles, "Please Please Me."** The stereo version has a different and inferior lead vocal. John Lennon sings the wrong words on the second line of the last verse and begins the next line with a suppressed chuckle, as if he's realized he's goofed.

→ **The Beatles, "Helter Skelter."** The "White Album" mono version runs a full 53 seconds shorter than the more familiar stereo one, with numerous differences in the drumming, guitar, and vocal, as well as some beeping noises not heard in the stereo version.

→ **The Who, "Our Love Was Is."** This stellar *The Who Sell Out* track has a whimsical slide guitar in the mono solo, as opposed to the superior and more familiar harder-rocking one in stereo.

→ **Pink Floyd, "Interstellar Overdrive."** An entire track with Rick Wright's keyboards is missing from the beginning of the stereo mix of this instrumental on their classic first album, *The Piper at the Gates of Dawn.*

→ **The Velvet Underground, "Some Kinda Love."** Not a stereo-mono difference, but entirely different mixes of The Velvet Underground's self-titled third album were issued in the United States and United Kingdom in 1969. The quieter mix, now known as "the closet mix," came out in the United States and has an entirely different take of "Some Kinda Love" with a hoarser vocal and just one guitar (where the U.K. mix has two). *–R.U.*

and power of the U.K. Atlantic pressing of 'Green Onions' when he heard it in a club."

POST-1960S AUDIOPHILE FORMATS

With the 12-inch stereo LP firmly entrenched as the most popular format for recorded music as the 1970s began, the industry looked for more ways to improve the sonic experience and, at least to some cynical observers, generate more profit with more expensive technologies. Some of these experiments were mixed successes at best and kind of disastrous at worst.

The most notorious failure might have been attempts to make records with quadraphonic sound, increasing the number of channels from two to four. Customers proved more reluctant to upgrade their equipment from stereo to the more expensive quadraphonic than from mono to stereo. Perhaps more crucially, quadraphonic pressings often didn't sound that good.

Technical explanations for the problematic quadraphonic processes could fill a book or two, so it might be best to give engineer Ron Nevison's explanation as to why The Who's 1973 double LP rock opera *Quadrophenia*, originally intended (as the title signifies, despite spelling "quadrophenia" with an "o") to be quadraphonic, came out in plain stereo: "When we tried a test mix halfway through with the album—when we finally got the equipment to encode these bullsh*t quad tracks—we realized that the front-to-back separation was like 5dB [decibels]. It was like a big giant mono."

In other words, listeners playing the album would hear far less difference between the channels than could be heard in the four-channel mixes created in the studio. There would be little

↑ Alec Palao has compiled, annotated, and produced hundreds of reissues. "There is no doubt that, with the occasional exception, you will invariably get better sound on the first or initial pressings of a record, particularly in relation to 1960s and 1970s releases," he advises.

to distinguish the sound coming out of the two rear speakers from the sound emanating from the two normal stereo front ones. The left-right separation between speakers on a typical home stereo at the time would have been in the 70–80dB range; by comparison, the front-to-back quadraphonic separation of 5dB was puny.

While it straddles the territory between artwork and the actual vinyl, picture discs—almost as old a feature as the commercial record itself—became more common in the 1970s after 10,000 picture discs were pressed of the 1970 *Airconditioning* LP by the British progressive rock band Curved Air. Countless picture discs have followed, on everything from a Three Stooges record to a Yardbirds interview disc (and that was just by one label, Rhino). Picture discs have generated countless collectibles, but more for the artwork than for the listening. Because they compress more material, picture discs usually boast infamously inferior fidelity to standard vinyl pressings. They're more likely to be appreciated as wall decorations than played, though the sonic deficiencies on spoken-word picture discs will at least be less annoying.

More successful, though geared toward a small audiophile niche market, were half speed masters. As the term implies, these are discs mastered at half speed, cut on the mastering lathe at 16⅔rpm, with the source

→ **Print ads of the 1970s target a growing class of home audio enthusiasts.**

↑ Prominent disco DJ Jellybean Benitez. The 12-inch single enabled DJs to play one song for more minutes than a 7-inch disc could usually hold, but also at greater fidelity, especially when cranked.

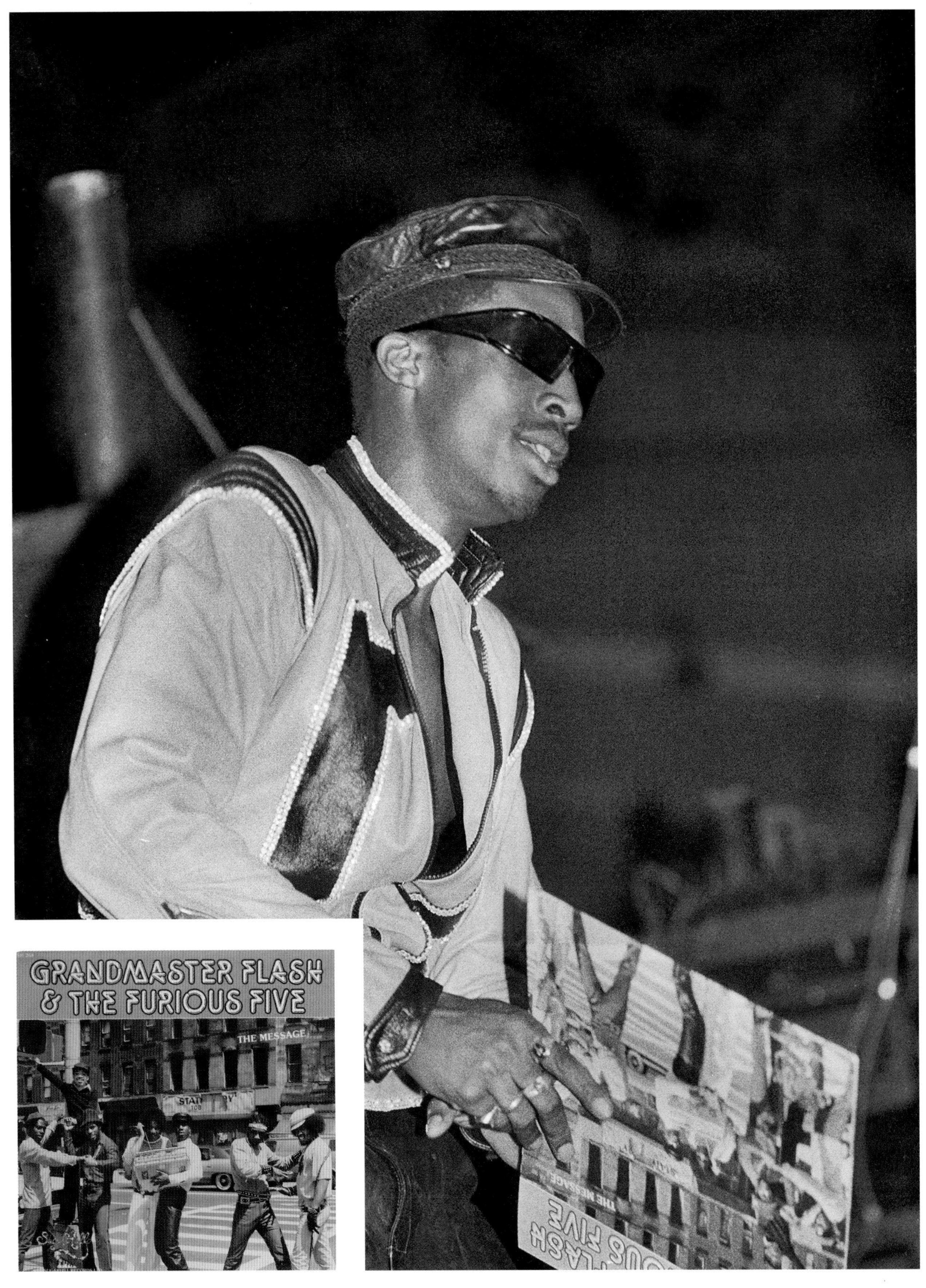
GRANDMASTER FLASH
& THE FURIOUS FIVE
THE MESSAGE

material (whether analog tape or, to the consternation of some audiophiles, digital) also slowed down to half speed. The idea is to make the sound richer, since it's easier to cut from midrange sound than from high-frequency sound.

While not everyone can tell a huge difference, enough listeners have maintained a market for half-speed-mastered LPs since the late 1970s, when Mobile Fidelity started to offer them on "Original Master Recording" albums. The market might always be limited, since half-speed masters are quite a bit more expensive than standard vinyl LPs. Mobile Fidelity's reputation also took a hit when it was revealed in 2022 that they had been using digital files in production, though customers had thought they were only using original master tapes.

One modification that did catch on, however, wasn't audiophile-only in nature. By the late 1970s, 12-inch singles were gaining in popularity in dance clubs, especially for disco records. They enabled DJs to play one song for more minutes than a 7-inch disc could usually hold, but at greater fidelity, especially when cranked loud. Some radio stations and listeners who weren't avid club-goers liked the experience, too; and the format proved applicable beyond the disco era. Grandmaster Flash scored one of the first big rap hits in 1982 with a 12-inch disc of "The Message"; the following year post-punk/new wave band New Order hit their "Blue Monday" 12-inch disc.

By then, the 12-inch vinyl LP's supremacy was also being threatened by prerecorded cassettes. While those would eventually fall into near disuse, the CD surpassed vinyl in sales by the 1990s and threatened the vinyl LP (and all vinyl releases) with extinction. So did the gradual rise of streaming. By 2006, according to the Nielsen Soundscan, just 900,000 such vinyl records were sold in the United States.

← **Grandmaster Flash at the UIC Pavilion in Chicago, Illinois, September 17, 1982. One of the first big hip-hop hits was Grandmaster Flash's 12-inch disc of "The Message."**

THE VINYL REVIVAL

Less than two decades later, of course, the tables have turned, with vinyl sales on a continual upward boom, 2021 marking their biggest year since 1986. The 12-inch LP must be considered a big part of that revival, as no other format—in the vinyl world or otherwise—offers such a large space for artwork, along with extras like LP-sized liner note booklets if labels wish. After years of near famine for consumers of new 12-inch LPs, now there's often a huge backup if labels want to press even a limited-edition vinyl release.

"I think the delays in the vinyl supply chain were, like with so many products, a result of the pandemic," says Gordon Anderson, copresident of Real Gone Music, which reissues numerous classic and collectible albums as vinyl LPs. "But it wasn't just that the raw materials to make records became difficult to procure. Folks cooped up at home definitely discovered the pleasures of good ol'-fashioned records, turbocharging demand well beyond what the already overstretched industry capacity could handle. With more plants and machines coming online, and a cooling in demand that is (unfortunately) already taking hold as households emerge from quarantine, I think the problem will ease in the coming months and years."

Yet for all the changes the 12-inch LP has been through, the process for making them remains the same. An aluminum acetate lacquer disc is made from the source recordings, whether tapes or digital files. A metal master disc is used to make a "mother," and vinyl is flattened between two stampers, each "stamped" with the basic info needed to press a vinyl LP. The number of copies pressed varies according to the order and demand, although, of course, these days it's rare for huge quantities of a single release to be pressed, let alone the millions that were done in the heydays of The Beatles, Pink Floyd, Fleetwood Mac, and Michael Jackson.

Many vinyl releases and reissues in the past couple decades have boasted 180-gram pressings for those who feel the thicker the disc, the better the sound and the more durable the content. Yet Gordon Anderson cautions, "Count me as a skeptic. There is nothing magical about 180-gram vinyl that offers better sound than regular vinyl. The only thing 180-gram vinyl offers is that it does

→ A shopper flips through the stacks at the XXVII International Record Fair of Barcelona. After years of near famine for consumers of new 12-inch LPs, there's now often a manufacturing backup if labels want to press even limited-edition vinyl releases.

The Cure
Room At The Top EP
Studio Outtakes
james
II
adolescent sex
JAPAN
THE CATCH
borderline
THE STAIRS
DANCE
PUNK/DISCO €1.00
70's/80's €1.00
PUNK/MOD/NEW WAVE
1 = €2.00
NEW STOCK
SALE INDIE 45's
SIOUXSIE AND THE BANSHEES / CREATURES
SEX PISTOLS / PUBLIC IMAGE LTD
PUNK/MOD/NEW WAVE
1 = €2.00

limit warpage. But I think the industry and consumers would be better served if more money was invested in improving packing materials to keep vinyl pristine for both business-to-business and business-to-consumer vinyl shipments rather than plunking down an extra three to five bucks for a 180-gram vinyl record that chews up more petroleum and increases freight costs."

As petroleum is part of PVC production, enthusiasts should be cautioned that the supply of vinyl records can be hampered by disruptions in the global oil-supply chain. Such was the case during the 1973 oil embargo, when The Who's double LP *Quadrophenia* was reportedly delayed (if only slightly) because of a vinyl shortage. Many records of the time were pressed with diluted concentrations of PVC, resulting in thinner LPs that could almost be wobbled like flexidiscs.

The environmental impact of manufacturing vinyl discs is an oft-overlooked byproduct of the form's revival, though it's discussed in a 2020 documentary about vinyl records and the stores that sell them, *Vinyl Nation*. "For all the (deserved) romance we have around vinyl, a record is petroleum-based plastic enrobed in cardboard then shipped around the globe on the power of fossil fuel," points out the film's codirector/coproducer, Kevin Smokler. "Pressing plants and labels are getting so much better at using regrind for records and recycled paper for sleeves, and, on the whole, we are simply making far fewer records than a half-century ago. But until we shrink the resource loop on record-making, the best way to not have your records be the eco-equivalent of an SUV idling in the driveway is to buy used records and keep them spinning and out of landfills for as long as the universe allows."

Even with those uncertainties, an ever-increasing wealth of consumers want—even demand—their product on vinyl, sometimes with heavier weights that many people feel ensure superior sound quality. For $400 to $500, there are even super-limited-edition reissues of 300 or fewer copies by the Electric Recording Company using 1950s valve tape machines for the disc cutting, among other diligently restored vintage equipment. For a technology scoffed at as obsolescent in the not-so-distant past, vinyl shows signs of outlasting every format for the dedicated music lover. ◊

↑ For a technology scoffed at as obsolescent in the not-so-distant past, vinyl shows signs of outlasting every format for the dedicated music lover.

ICONIC **COVERS**

THERE'S A RIOT GOIN' ON • SLY AND THE FAMILY STONE

Influential on later covers into the CD age, *There's a Riot Goin' On* is distinctive due to its lack of any text but also the bold alterations made to the American flag. The stars were replaced by suns because Sly thought that stars implied searching (and, implicitly, frustration). But his overarching idea was to unite all colors, with white representing absence of color, red suggesting our shared blood, and black (substituted for the usual blue) representing all colors combined. –M.P.

DROPPING THE NEEDLE

TURNTABLES AND OTHER HI-FI EQUIPMENT

BY KEN MICALLEF

↑ Through all of vinyl's ups and downs, one thing has remained constant: The vinyl experience enables full music engagement and requires full emotional, mental, and intellectual attention.

True believers and analog newcomers alike concur: Vinyl is back in a way the world hasn't seen since the late 1980s, when compact discs were heralded for their "perfect sound forever." How did they get it so wrong when we got it so right? Owning vinyl and a turntable is now commonplace, even fashionable, as depicted in popular TV shows, films, and advertisements for luxury goods and common household fare. New LPs (for long-player, *not* "vinyls"!) are sold in small towns and large cities around the globe. When a new recording is released, the ubiquitous streaming option most often is accompanied by its vinyl counterpart, including glorious, full-sized cover art, liner notes, and sometimes even a download code and unique tracks not available in any other format.

The road from there to here is a fascinating one and has its origins way back in the 1870s, when Thomas Edison began tinkering with primitive sound devices. His invention would spawn the first flat disc–reading machine by German immigrant Emile Berliner (and his playback "Gramophone"), which over the following century would spawn a multimillion-dollar business for sound-engraved polyvinyl chloride discs and the machines that play them.

One thing remains constant: The vinyl experience enables full music engagement and requires full emotional, mental, and intellectual attention. Unlike streaming files, which can become unobtrusive background music, vinyl records insist on full attention and give commensurate rewards in listening pleasure.

The following chapter includes a brief historical progression of vinyl discs and turntables; a deep dive into turntable technology; how turntables work with other components of the analog sound-producing system chain; and, finally, an overview of luxury record spinners, everyday record players, all-in-one machines, and fashionable consoles designed to capture your listening pleasure and interior design sense.

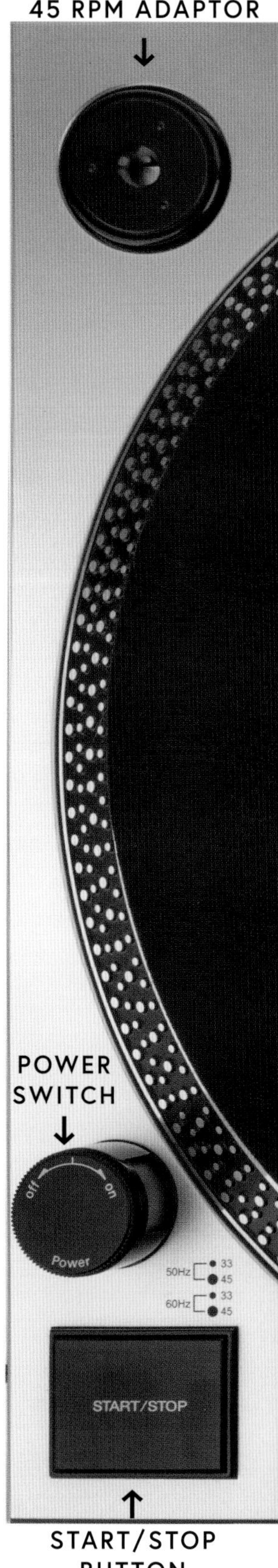

SPINDLE
PLINTH (BASE)
COUNTERWEIGHT
PLATTER
ANTI-SKATE CONTROL
CUE LEVER
ARM REST
TONEARM
PITCH ADJUSTMENT
PITCH ADJ.
CARTRIDGE
SPEED
33
45
STYLUS (NOT VISIBLE)
TARGET LIGHT
MAT
STYLUS LIGHT
SPEED SELECTOR

TURNTABLE COMPONENTS: WHAT MAKES A RECORD PLAYER SING

Whether it's a luxury high-end machine or an inexpensive entry-level record player, all turntables share the same constituent parts. You could say that these elements *define* a turntable, whether owned by analog purists, high-end audio devotees (a.k.a. "audiophiles"), or a newbie record collector intent on coveting (a) all four colored vinyl discs of Taylor Swift's *Midnights*, (b) the complete Atlantic/Prestige/Impulse! works of jazz tenor saxophonist John Coltrane, or (c) Jay Z's *The Black Album*. If the following electromechanical elements don't exist, a turntable is no more an analog playback machine than a CD player.

The six parts common to all turntables include the cartridge/styli; tonearm with counterweight; platter with mat; record spindle; plinth or base; and motor, which drives the platter. In addition, most turntables include a set of three or four feet (sometimes adjustable), a small cueing lever to lift the tonearm and gently lower the cartridge's stylus into the record's lead-in groove, a dust-cover, and a clamp to tighten the record to the platter and thus flatten possible warpage while bringing the record into closer relationship with the platter for better tracking. Typically, a speed selector controls playback speed (45, 33, and sometimes 78rpm). Some 1950s and 1960s analog machines include a brake to quickly start/stop the platter/record, a necessity at all analog radio stations and DJ booths.

STYLUS: DIAMOND IN THE GROOVE

Each part of the turntable has a specific role to play in creating its sound and reproducing the music we love. The phono cartridge's stylus, or needle, typically a diamond, tracks the V-shaped grooves of the vinyl disc, converting its engraved modulations into electrical impulses, or voltage. Different types of sound are produced by different diamond shapes, typically conical, elliptical, or fine-line varieties. The electrical impulses/voltage generated by the stylus are translated and amplified by the cartridge's magnet or metal coils.

PHONO CARTRIDGES: COMPLEX ELECTROMECHANICAL DEVICES

The interior elements of the cartridge, or "cart," the body of which is usually made of plastic (until you get to more expensive models), include the suspension and cantilever (which holds the stylus); the coils or magnet, which amplify

→ Tiny electrical signals are the beginning of the journey that produces analog sound. The electrical signal generated by the stylus and phono cartridge must be preamplified before meeting the main amplification stage of an integrated amplifier or receiver.

the signal from the stylus; and four small output pins at the back of the cart (marked left/positive, right/positive, two negative).

Tiny electrical signals are the beginning of the journey that produces analog sound. The electrical signal generated by a phono cartridge creates a small signal that is equally low in volume, much lower than a compact disc signal. That tiny signal must be preamplified before meeting the main amplification stage of an integrated amplifier or receiver, be it solid-state, tubed, or Class-D. If you want the highly detailed, large-scale, lifelike experience of an audiophile, a choice of separate solid-state or tube amplification is the ultimate option. Solid-state or class-D amplifiers (a class-D amplifier, or switching amplifier, uses transistors operating as electronic switches, not as linear gain devices as in other amplifiers). A cart's volume level will also depend on whether it's a moving magnet (MM) or moving coil (MC) type. In an MM cart, the signal from the stylus causes its internal magnet to vibrate and produce signal. In an MC cart, the magnet is static, while the internal coils move to produce signal. MC carts are typically lighter in weight and use finer wire, making them more sensitive to stylus tracking—and more expensive than MM carts (often with a more nuanced sound). However, both types can produce very good sound.

REMARKABLE **RECORD STORES**

HMV (HIS MASTER'S VOICE) • *LONDON, ENGLAND*

HMV's flagship store opened in the center of London's shopping district on Oxford Street in 1921, with composer Sir Edgar Elgar on hand as celebrity guest. Its wide-ranging selection made it a must-stop destination for every discerning music fan. In 1986 the shop relocated to a new Oxford Street location, which they boasted made them the largest record store in the world. It moved back to its original location in the new century before closing in 2019. –*G.G.*

↑ In use since the 1930s, the main purpose of a tonearm remains the same: to align the cartridge with the vinyl on the platter, part of an all-in-one system with critical setup parameters.

THE TONEARM: TURNTABLE WORKHORSE

Tonearms are 9, 10, 11, or 12 inches long and typically made of aluminum or carbon fiber. Tonearms employ different designs, such as gimbal or uni-pivot, depending on how they are attached to the turntable's plinth and the sonic goals of the designer.

Though in use since the 1930s, the main purpose of a tonearm remains the same: to align the cartridge with the vinyl on the platter, part of an all-in-one system with critical setup parameters. The four pins of the cartridge attach to the tonearm wires, which stream through its hollow main tube, terminating in a pair of interconnects that attach to the input connections of a phono preamplifier, amplifier, or receiver. The tonearm pivot point, at the back of the turntable, includes a collar, bearing, and cueing arm set into a base. At the very back of the tonearm, a rotating metal counterweight dials in the correct tracking weight for the cartridge, as determined by its manufacturer. Setting tracking weight below the manufacturer's recommendation can cause the stylus to jump and may damage your record, and you won't hear all the information in the vinyl grooves. If tracking force is too heavy, you might hear distortion or cause damage known as "groove wear," which may be visible on the record's soft and malleable material.

← Often the heaviest part of the turntable, platters are typically made of aluminum, although glass, copper, steel, ceramic, wood, and acrylic have been used, as in the case of this McIntosh MT10 turntable's outsized platter.

PLATTER: STEEL WHEELS

The platter is the large, circular-shaped disc that dominates the appearance of the turntable and spins the record. Often the heaviest part of the turntable, platters are typically made of aluminum (although glass, copper, steel, ceramic, even wood and composite materials have been used), as well as various damping materials to quiet and stabilize the platter. In some older playback machines (for instance, 1957's Thorens TD 124), a rubber-matted aluminum shell covers the main platter. Very expensive modern turntables use multiple platters or even platters running in opposite directions for stability, speed correction, or other sonic benefits.

The spindle is the small metal post that juts up from the center of the platter, establishing a connection point for the record. The spindle spins on a small bearing beneath the platter, typically treated with a light oil. One problem of buying vintage turntables is the condition of the bearing, which is unknown, given the lack of knowledge about who previously owned the table and how it was treated. The spindle bearings, as well as those at the base of the tonearm assembly, must be in good shape for the turntable to operate smoothly, at the correct speed, and without noise.

MOTOR: THE ENGINE INSIDE

An AC or DC motor drives the platter by various means: via a rubber belt which wraps around a pulley atop the motor to the platter, direct drive (i.e., a motor attached to the platter), or rim or idler drives that move the platter in conjunction with wheels or pulleys driven by a motor. Motors are installed directly below the platter, outside the platter, or even outside the turntable if the designer believes isolating the motor is key to noise reduction. There are as many theories about turntable motors as there are turntables. Some believe that belt-driven motors create a more rhythmically adept, smoother, quieter sound, while fans of old-school idler drives favor their dynamics and punch.

↑ An AC or DC motor drives the platter by various means, usually via a rubber belt or direct drive, i.e., a motor attached to the platter.

ICONIC **COVERS**

NEW YORK DOLLS

NEW YORK DOLLS

Design house Album Graphics, Inc.; photographer Toshi; hairstylist Shin; and makeup artist Dave O'Grady collaborate with the always-willing Dolls to create an incendiary image of the band as thuggish cross-dressers. Fact is, hair metal didn't get its fashion sense from Ziggy Stardust—they got it from Johnny Thunders. *–M.P.*

REEL TO REEL

The standard for music recording from the 1930s through the 1980s, reel-to-reel magnetic tape was also a successful commercial medium throughout the 1960s, purchased by those looking for the absolute best in high fidelity playback. “Multitracking” to tape allowed musicians to record multiple instruments or vocals over the original recorded performance (“overdubbing”), the master tape then available for further editing in a tape-equipped studio of the musician or producer’s choice. Reel-to-reel tape surrendered its supremacy in retail, first, to 8-track, then cassettes, compact discs, finally, streaming. Digital recording became the norm in the 1990s. The reel-to-reel format experienced a revival in popularity among audiophiles in the 2000s, although new production of tape reels and playback machines has largely ceased.

Reel-to-reel tape was popular among recording engineers for its ability to be physically spliced and re-edited, creating a unique mix dependent on either the producer or musician’s intents. As experimentation increased, tape was manipulated by all manner of effects, from doubling or delaying sounds (Jamaican “dub”) to creating entire tape collages. The Beatles famously spun tape reels held aloft by pencils in “Tomorrow Never Knows” and created an entire tape symphony in “Revolution No 9.” Tape experiments prior to The Beatles included classical composers from Karlheinz Stockhausen (“Hymnen”) and Otto Luening and Vladimir Ussachevsky (Tape Music An Historic Concert) to John Cage (“Williams Mix”).

Reel to reel remains the preferred recording format for musicians hoping to achieve a warmer or more “tape saturated sound”; analog tape (often for drums) and digital recording now coexist side by side in many professional recording studios. *–K.M.*

THE PLINTH: BLOCK THEORY

The plinth or base of the turntable is as important to good sound as the tonearm, cartridge, platter, and motor. There are many theories as to what constitutes the best plinth. Roy Gandy, CEO of Rega Ltd., believes the lightest plinth is ideal, as it's better able to release stored resonances or vibrations, which can muddy and distort sound. Others, like Harry Weisfeld (VPI Industries) and Franc Kuzma (Kuzma Ltd.) apply mass to deaden resonances. Older Thorens, Garrard, Empire, Fairchild, and AR tables fall somewhere between modern approaches. The top-of-the-line Rega Planar 10 Reference weighs little more than 10 pounds. Kuzma's ultimate, bronze-attired XL Air clocks in at 265 pounds.

↑ A turntable with a wood plinth. There are many theories as to the most effective material and mass for the plinth.

SETUP TO ACHIEVE ULTIMATE TURNTABLE FIDELITY

Arguably more important than any other element of a high-fidelity audio chain, turntable setup is crucial. This can be a frustrating and tricky business—patience rewards with the best sound. Professional cart/tonearm alignment is suggested and possibly mandatory.

A cartridge can be screwed into a universal headshell, such as that on the Technics SL-1200 turntable (but originating with Swedish company SME). Universal headshells afford the easiest setup, as the cartridge can first be affixed to the headshell, which is then screwed into the tonearm's adjustable collar. Connecting and aligning a cart to a static headshell (part of the tonearm) requires a greater degree of skill and experience. Again, consulting a pro is a wise move.

A protractor aligns the cartridge to the tonearm, following one of three alignment scenarios developed by 1950s designers Baerwald, Stevenson, and Lundgren. Inexpensive turntables usually include a perfectly usable paper protractor, or one can be downloaded from the popular Vinyl Engine website (vinylengine.com). Expensive turntables from Acoustic Signature, VPI, and others include a metal alignment jig. The Dr. Feickert Next

↓ Setting the turntable's tracking force is just one step in properly calibrating for optimum playback. Beware, however, of inexpensive scales commonly available on eBay and elsewhere. Riverstone's gauge, at $33, is an affordable and reliable option.

ICONIC **COVERS**

THE DARK SIDE OF THE MOON • PINK FLOYD

One of rock's most recognizable images, the refracting prism on the cover of Pink Floyd's eighth album, can be enjoyed infinitely—its beams continue onto the back and inside the gate, lining up with a second butted-up copy and a third etc. Hipgnosis also reinforced the triangle motif with a pyramid poster and stylized pyramid stickers. *–M.P.*

REMARKABLE **RECORD STORES**

WATERLOO RECORDS • *AUSTIN, TEXAS*

This shop has been integral not just to Austin's own lively music scene but also in its strong support of Texas music in general. Waterloo opened in 1982 and soon found itself almost in as much demand as a live venue as it did a record store, especially after the South by Southwest music conference launched in 1987 and Waterloo in-stores became a mainstay of the event. Musician Alejandro Escovedo still likes to boast, "I was the greatest employee Waterloo ever had." –*G.G.*

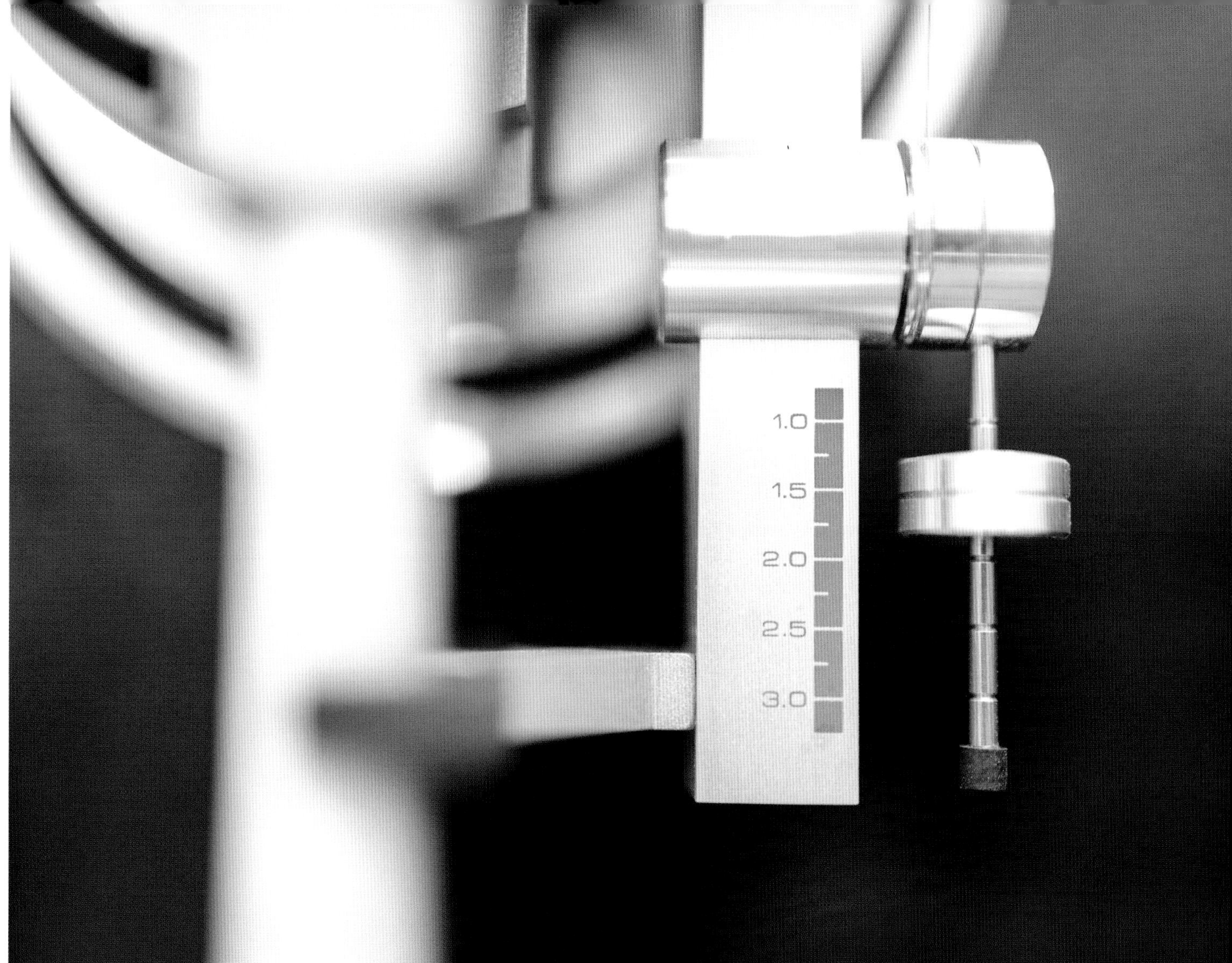

↑ **A counterweight at the back of the tonearm is used to set the tracking force of the stylus.**

Generation Cartridge Alignment Tool, WAM Engineering WallyTractor Universal v2.01, and Pro-Ject Align It are ideal for state-of-the-art professional alignment setups.

Dialing in cartridge tracking force as dictated by the manufacturer is best achieved not with an inexpensive electronic gauge bought on eBay (they're often weighted incorrectly) but by acquiring an easy-to-use device like the professional-level Riverstone Audio Record-Level Turntable Stylus Tracking Force Gauge/Scale, currently available for about $33 online.

Azimuth refers to the perpendicular angle of the cartridge required for optimal cartridge-to-record tracking so as to track equally both sides of the record grooves. Ideally a 90-degree angle is desired. Inexpensive turntable/tonearm combos don't offer azimuth adjustment, a standard option on more expensive tonearms. For professionals, the electronic Musical Surroundings Fozgometer V2 meter is the last word in obtaining perfect azimuth. But like the title of the Norman Mailer novel, correct azimuth adjustment can be a "spooky art," with many opposing opinions as to what constitutes correct adjustment.

VTA, or vertical tracking angle, is easier to understand and implement. Some turntables offer a small screw set in the tonearm base, which allows up or down movement of the arm tube. Typically setting the tonearm parallel to the platter surface will produce the most even sound. If the sound is bright, the tonearm should be lowered at its base, hopefully adjusting the tonal focus from bright to more midrange or bass energized. The key here is listening and trusting your ears.

Finally turntables are *very* sensitive to motion, vibration, and external noise. It's essential to place the turntable on a solid platform (a bamboo board such as Ikea's APTITLIG is a popular and inexpensive solution), which helps isolate the turntable's delicate machinery. Turntables should *never* be placed on top of a loudspeaker, on the floor, or atop other components, as every vibration that passes through those surfaces will be translated to the turntable, where they can muddy, distort, and generally ruin the very delicate signals generated by the cartridge/stylus. A turntable must be level, as determined by a carpenter's level or supplied level. If not level, the tonearm will track weighted to the left or the right side of the groove, creating record damage and audible distortion.

8 TRACK

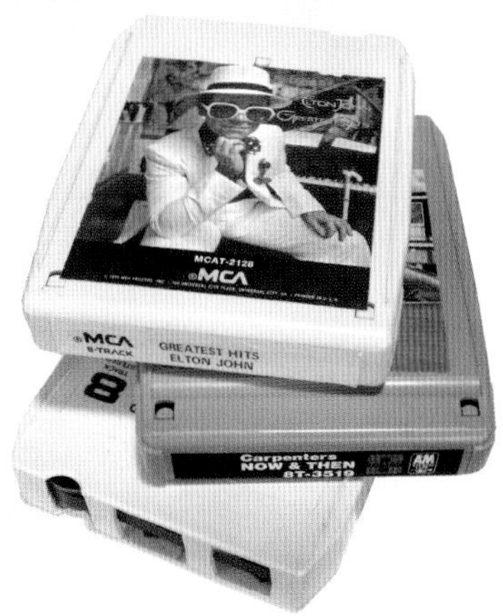

8-track tape will forever be synonymous with Chevy vans and waterbeds; music that squeaked, squawked, and dropped out as the tape stretched; and the format's chunky casework, which resembled a plastic paperback book.

The first music playback medium designed for the automobile, "tape decks" typically installed in or under the car dashboard. 8 tracks used magnetic tape ingrained with music information in much the same way as professional reel-to-reel recording tape, but of far lower quality within a similarly poor-quality plastic cartridge.

Included in Ford Motor Company's Mustang, Thunderbird, and Lincoln car models in 1965, 8-track cartridges had dimensions of 5.25 inches by 4 inches by 0.8 inches. Within its plastic shell, magnetic tape was rolled around a single spool, and comprised eight parallel tracks. The tape player's head read two of these tracks simultaneously, achieving stereo sound. When a song was completed, the tape head moved to another set of two tracks, making a distinctive clicking noise, like a flipping metal turnstile.

8-track machines for the home were introduced in 1966, allowing music lovers to share tapes between their homes, automobiles, and portable players. By the late 1960s, 8 tracks nearly dominated music sales; soon, prerecorded releases on 8 track hit stores within a month of the vinyl release.

Sales of 8-track tapes nosedived after their 1978 peak, replaced by the music cassette. *–K.M.*

TURNTABLES AND TURNTABLE SYSTEMS: A BRIEF HISTORY

Today's turntables originated from a large horn affixed to a needle that tracked a cylinder engraved with musical modulations. The engravings read by the needle were translated as sound flowing out of the expanding mouth of the horn. Thomas Edison's Edison Home Model A (1903) and Eugène Ducretet's Tinfoil Phonograph (1881) preceded the first instance of a needle reading a disc on a platter on Emile Berliner's Berliner Gramophone (1893–1896). Larger machines followed, including Victor's 6 Phonograph (1900s), Victor's Portable Gramophone (1915), and Pathé's Model D and Coquet Phonograph (1903).

Entering the electric era, Victor Talking Machine Company's Orthophonic Victrola Credenza (1925) may have been the first console system, with a hand crank to power its hidden turntable. Portables followed, including the Mikiphone Pocket Phonograph, HMV Model 101, Thorens Excelda Portable Gramophone, and RCA's Special Model N. By the 1940s, shellac spinning was common, hence Wilcox-Gay Corporation's popular A95 and Wurlitzer's Model 1015 jukebox (1946). Dual's 1000 record player featured a motor shaft with a worm-drive tip, which engaged a platter shaft with corresponding mesh worm gear.

The birth of high fidelity (a.k.a. "hi-fi") and the modern turntable kicked off in the 1950s, with Fairchild's 412 (1950s); Luxor's RTW6; Braun's sleek, minimalist PC 3 Record Player (1956); and Atelier 1-81 Compact Stereo Sound System. As record players took off in the marketplace, designs that followed included the chunky, 45rpm-only

↑ Opera singer Enrico Caruso listens back to his customized Victrola.

→ Waldman's Record Shop in New York City, circa 1920, displays Victrolas in wood cabinets. The shop is decorated with the Victor Records' mascot (top left and right) and photos of top recording artists of the day, including Enrico Caruso.

REMARKABLE **RECORD STORES**

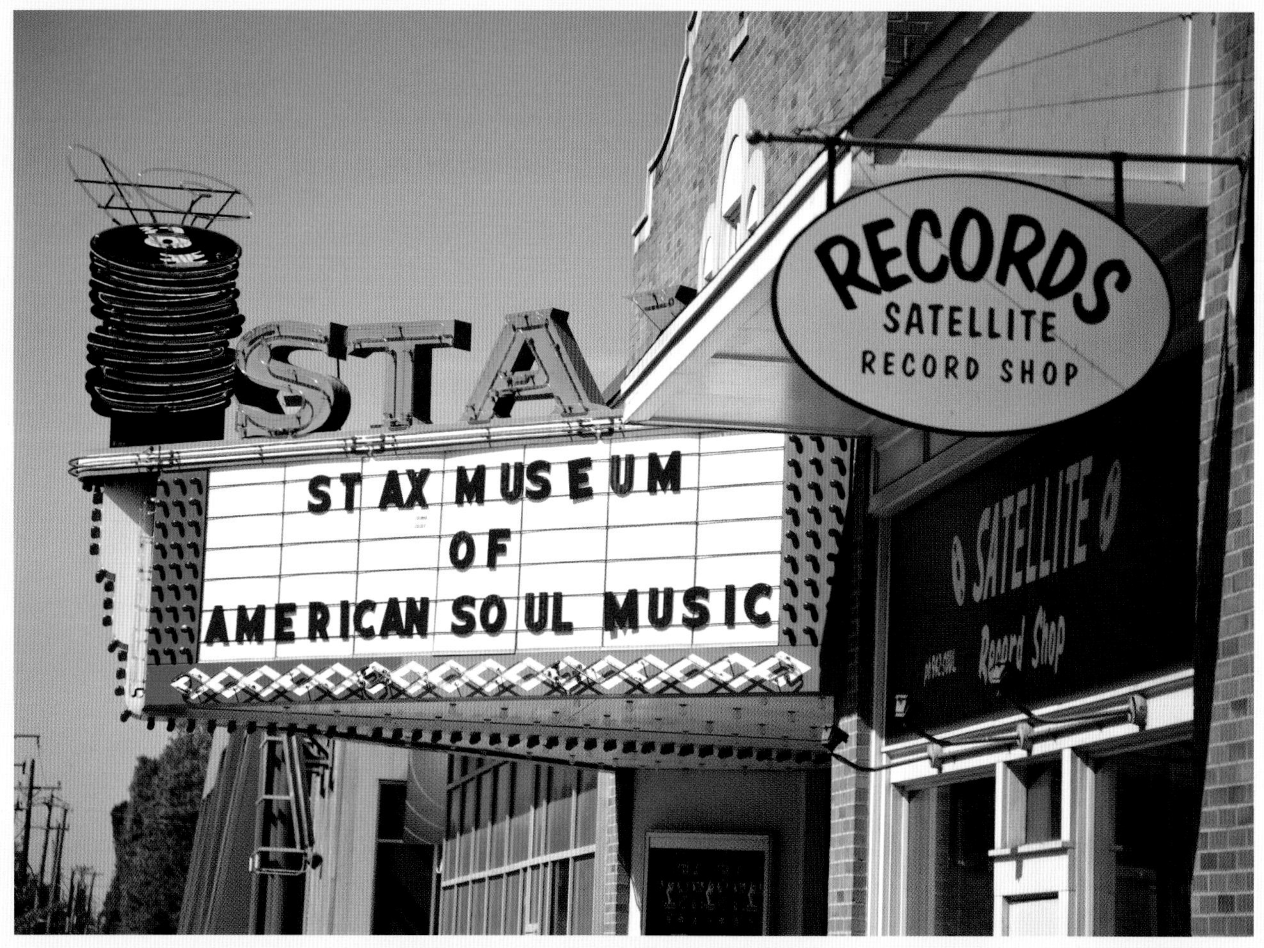

SATELLITE RECORD SHOP • *MEMPHIS, TENNESSEE*

When Stax Studios moved to 926 East McLemore in 1960, the Satellite Record Shop opened in the same building, a former movie theater. It quickly became a hangout for the cream of Southern soul musicians who passed through the studio's doors. The studio and store closed in 1975. Then in 2003 the site was reborn as the Stax Museum of American Soul Music—with the Satellite Record Shop still right next door. *–G.G.*

↑ Though not exactly audiophile-quality, inexpensive portable players of the 1950s and 1960s served as gateways to more desirable gear for countless music lovers.

RCA 45EY; ELAC's sleek Bingo Miraphon; the fantastical, Space Age–inspired Kuba Komet Entertainment Centre (including a pull-out, four-speed Telefunken phonograph); the techy-looking Joboton 712; Garrard's streamlined 4HF; and the portable Philips AG2100 Mignon Automobile Turntable and Metz Babyphon 56 Kofferradio.

Radio stations and recording studios required industrial-strength players, employing Thorens' TD 124 (my turntable of choice, with a Jelco arm), EMT's (Elektromesstechnik) 927 (1953), Garrard's 301 (1954), and the Rek-O-Kut T-12H Exclusive (1950s), all of which are still sought after by fans of vintage machines, as are Danish company Ortofon's highly regarded cartridges and tonearms. Grundig's Majestic 9070 Console debuted in 1958, featuring an enclosed turntable and reel-to-reel tape deck hidden behind curved doors. The 1950s were also a popular time for portable players, including Dansette's Popular Portable Record Player, Decca's Portable Record Player, and Philips's Phonokoffer III Record Player (1953).

The 1960s brought refined turntable designs and more adaptable tonearms and cartridges. The revolutionary Acoustic Research (AR) XA (1961) innovated a decoupled, isolated suspension, an early belt-drive approach, and lightweight platter. Other popular models included the Garrard 401, Goldring Lenco GL75, Sugden Connoisseur, portable Newcomb TR-1625M, the stunning Rek-O-Kut Rondine B-12H, ERA Bloc Source Quarante, and further models from Braun, Dual, ELAC, and Thorens. Innovative tonearms from Grace and SME, and cartridges from Shure and Grado, populated an increasingly heated market for audio components.

Manufacturers became as interested in design as sound during the 1970s, resulting in Bang & Olufsen's stylish Beogram 1102 with MMC 020 S Cartridge (1976), Denon's DP-3000 (1972), and candy-colored portables from Europhon and Philips. Linn, Rabco, Revox, and Thorens introduced players with sophisticated tonearms and cartridges built for the burgeoning audiophile market, while high-quality mass-market models—including Kenwood's JD-500 (1975), JVC's QL-7 (1977), and Pioneer's PL-570 (1976)—flooded living rooms from London to Los Angeles. Trendy all-on-one, groovy designs included the Wega Studio 3231 and Rosita Stereo Commander Luxus; more serious 1970s offerings included Garrard's Zero 100c, ADC Accutrac 4000, Dual 1229, and a *Star Trek*–inspired portable, the Weltron 2007. Ortofon continued its cartridge dominance, with newcomer Supex (later Koetsu) introducing then exotic materials like cerium cobalt magnets, high-purity metals, and polished elliptical styli.

The 1980s and 1990s brought heavier materials and more exotic tonearms and carts in an era of luxury turntables employing NASA-worthy designs. Alternately Technics' SL-1200 MK started a revolution in DJ machines, its popularity unabated today. Forsell, Sota, Audioméca, Nottingham, Goldmund, Luxman, Oracle, Micro Seiki, Sony, and VPI Industries introduced massive machines for well-heeled vinyl lovers, gratifying them with "black backgrounds," giant soundstages, and highly detailed productions. Exciting cartridge and tonearm designs similarly accelerated. Audio-Technica created their popular AT727 Sound Burger portable; Revox's B791 offered a servo-controlled,

LEGENDARY **LABELS**

MOTOWN

No other record label, major or independent, has as strong a global identity as Motown. The Detroit company helped define soul music with an incredible wealth of 1960s hits by The Miracles, The Supremes, The Temptations, Mary Wells, Martha and the Vandellas, The Marvelettes, The Four Tops, Stevie Wonder, Marvin Gaye, Gladys Knight & the Pips, and The Jackson 5. These rolled out with almost factory-like precision from Berry Gordy Jr.'s operation on Motown and an assortment of subsidiary labels, including Tamla, Gordy, and V.I.P. While the label continued to score hits after moving to Los Angeles in the early 1970s, it lost much of the distinctive R&B/pop/gospel mixture that's made many records identifiable as Motown product to millions of listeners who don't even collect records. *–R.U.*

CASSETTE

Perhaps the beginning of truly portable, personal stereo sound after the 1960s transistor radio, prerecorded and blank analog cassettes ("Compact Cassette") were aided by the explosion in sales of the Sony Walkman cassette player, which could be strapped on a belt or arm, providing sturdy playback whether the listener was lounging, running, or traveling. Originally used in dictation machines, improvements in fidelity saw the cassette replace 8 track and reel-to-reel formats in consumer environments in the 1970s. Three of the biggest selling cassettes included Pink Floyd's *The Dark Side of the Moon* (1973), Michael Jackson's *Thriller* (1982), and Nirvana's *Nevermind* (1991). Following the vinyl resurgence in the mid-2000s, cassettes also experienced a revival, some collectors valuing them for their prerecorded mixes of 70s and 80s music.

A miniaturized version of a professional recording tape reel, plastic cassettes held two miniature spools, through which magnetic tape passed. The spools and other internal mechanisms worked together inside the oblong plastic shell, measuring 4 inches by 2.5 inches by 0.5 inches. Cassette tapes contained music signal on both sides of the tape, and could be reversed, rewound, and advanced (fast forward). *–K.M.*

parallel tracking tonearm; tape deck manufacturer Nakamichi introduced the Dragon-CT. Wilson Benesch, EMT, and Roksan offered cutting-edge designs. While CDs reigned, the faithful held fast to their turntables, as if knowing the technology's rebirth was around the corner.

The current era has seen increased growth in opulent turntables from VPI, Acoustic Signature, Bergmann, Clearaudio, TechDAS, Döhmann, Wilson Benesch, Simon Yorke, and others, just as a resurgence of interest in vinyl exploded. As Rega Ltd. and Pro-Ject Audio Systems experienced an incredible surge in sales of both entry-level and high-end turntables, cartridges from Ortofon, Hana, Koetsu, Nagaoka, Audio-Technica, Benz Micro, Sumiko, Goldring, and others provided bang-for-the-buck prices at lower- to mid-tier carts, with multi-thousand-dollar offerings for carts with complex engineering and exotic parts.

We are experiencing a golden age of turntables, tonearms, and cartridges. Portables, all-in-one systems, Bluetooth-enabled models, both entry-level and high-end turntables, tonearms, and cartridges are available as never before. While brick-and-mortar audio stores haven't experienced rebirth, vinyl record stores exist in practically every town in North America, Europe, and the Far East. Turntables and vinyl can be found at mass-market electronic stores, clothing boutiques, flea markets, and department and hardware stores, with even greater choices available online.

ICONIC **COVERS**

BLUES FOR ALLAH

GRATEFUL DEAD

This stunning and frightening 1974 painting called *The Fiddler* earned Phillip Harris both the Gold Award and the Award of Merit from the Society of Illustrators. What it did for The Dead was help perpetuate the band's foreboding and even occult visual narrative, which was wholly incongruous with the good vibes put out through their hippie lyrics and generally happy musical ramblings. –*M.P.*

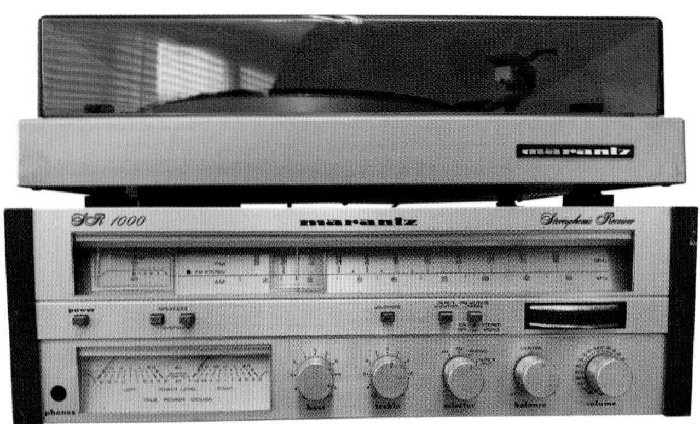

↑ The cartridge's low-level signal must be boosted to meet line-level standards. An integrated amplifier—a preamplifier and power amplifier rolled into one—can be driven by solid-state transistors (left) or vacuum tubes (right).

SYSTEM COMPONENTS AND HOW THEY WORK TOGETHER

While turntables are based on classic technology, today's models are anything but primitive. When you consider that many turntables are sold as part of an all-in-one, complete system, the prospects for creating a personalized system to meet your distinctive needs are practically boundless.

Whether buying a manual or automatic turntable (which returns the tonearm to its resting place after a side is completed), you can follow the separate components route, which offers the best overall sound and the highest cost. Basic turntables include a cartridge; more expensive models often don't. Basically a stand-alone turntable connects to a phono preamplifier (via a pair of interconnects addressing left and right channels), where the cartridge's low-level signal is boosted to meet line-level standards, further amplified by the preamplifier and power amplifier. The phono preamplifier can be incorporated into the turntable, sold separately, or as part of an integrated amplifier—a cryptic designation for a pre- and power amplifier rolled into one. Typically amplification is connected via a pair of cables to left and right speakers, signifying the start of your listening session.

You can also buy a system that includes a turntable built into a case that includes all necessary amplification, even speakers. This is essentially a throwback to the consoles of the 1950s. Console systems are often designed to look as good as they sound, sometimes better.

There are myriad choices for systems built around a turntable. There are Bluetooth-enabled turntables and systems. Going wireless is arguably

LEGENDARY **LABELS**

BLUE NOTE

Founded in 1939 by Alfred Lion and Max Margulis, Blue Note has been a big name in jazz recording since the birth of bop. Expanding into 10-inch and then 12-inch LPs in the early to mid-1950s, it's also esteemed by jazz buffs for its highly distinctive, cleanly designed covers, which exuded cool modernism just as much as the music they contained. It would take several pages to list the jazz icons who spent at least some time on Blue Note, including Thelonious Monk, Art Blakey, Herbie Hancock, Lee Morgan, Miles Davis, and Jimmy Smith. While Blue Note's 1950s and 1960s bop and cool classics might be its most highly regarded items, it continued to record new music and artists into the twenty-first century, scoring its biggest hits with Norah Jones's first albums. –*R.U.*

CD

Introduced in the early 1980s, the compact disc (CD) promised "Perfect Sound Forever," and largely banished vinyl albums as the music lover's medium of choice, until the omnipotence of streaming and the vinyl resurgence practically destroyed the market for CDs altogether. Though compact disc production has largely halted, millions of CD collections remain, perhaps awaiting *their* resurgence, which some believe has already arrived.

Standard CDs have a diameter of 120 millimeters (4.7 inches) and can hold up to 74 minutes of uncompressed digital audio, up to 80 minutes. A CD is made of 1.2-millimeter thick, polycarbonate plastic, and weighs 14–33 grams.

The compact disc spawned similarly sized discs that held various types of media; CD-ROM, CD Mini, Super Audio CD, Super Video CD, and Enhanced CD all came and went, eventually acquiescing popularity to easier to use digital files.

Plastic jewel cases that could break off into tiny shards, and the deficient artwork of CD cover art hastened its demise, even if sound quality (and the sound quality of compact disc players) improved near the end of the format's reign. *–K.M.*

not the road to high-quality sound, which requires wired connections. Vinyl playback is a physical medium that demands a physical relationship. Similarly you can purchase self-powered or "active" speakers, that require only a phono stage–equipped turntable—no other amplification required. Most complete systems include a headphone amp, or you can buy an outboard headphone amp with dedicated circuitry to get the best from your headphones.

If you want the highly detailed, large-scale, life-like experience of an audiophile, a choice of separate solid-state or tube amplification is the ultimate option. Solid-state or Class-D amplifiers ("a class-D amplifier or switching amplifier uses transistors, usually MOSFETs [metal–oxide–semiconductor field-effect transistors], operating as electronic switches, not as linear gain devices as in other amplifiers") offer the greatest power and often the deepest, tightest bass notes. Fans of tube amps laud their natural sound, a "soundstage" or "sound field" that "blooms" into your listening space, and instrumental and vocal tone that more closely resembles the live, original performance. Single-ended triode (SET)–based tube amps are the purest gateway to wholly natural sound, with their direct signal paths, lack of signal distorting features, and very hot-running power tubes arguably constituting the pinnacle of sound/music reproduction.

ICONIC **COVERS**

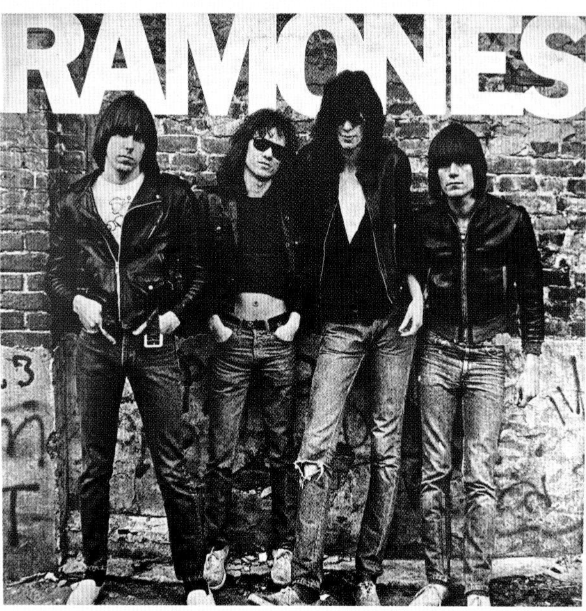

RAMONES

RAMONES

Punk magazine's Roberta Bayley (also part-time ticket-taker at CBGB) took this iconic photo of (left to right) Johnny, Tommy, Joey, and Dee Dee. It established the Ramones' trademark fashion sense, and as a bonus, the back cover represents the first work from the band's graphic artist Arturo Vega, who would create a fashion empire that far outstrips the band's impact in terms of record sales. *–M.P.*

TURNTABLES AT EVERY PRICE POINT

Before the vinyl resurgence, well-built entry-level tables were available only from established turntable manufacturers: England's Rega Ltd., Slovenia's Pro-Ject Audio Systems, Japan's Audio-Technica, New Jersey's VPI Industries, or the ever-popular used option from Japan, a Technics SL-1000. (As noted earlier, used turntables can present a bevy of problems not found in new units). If well cared for, these turntables can last a lifetime and offer the same basic options as more expensive tables.

As vinyl and turntables have grown in popularity, inexpensive stand-alone turntables have hit the market, as well as lifestyle turntables, 45rpm-only turntables, consoles, turntables that play underwater or play while hanging vertically, turntables with levitating platters, a turntable built into a conga drum, and complete packaged systems from turntable-centric dealers.

Though it has stiff competition, the U-Turn Orbit Basic—a crowdfunded design that became available in 2008 roughly at the same time when the vinyl resurgence began—is a solid record spinner for less than $200.

Well-made turntables in the $500 range include the Pro-Ject Audio Systems T1 Phono SB (includes built-in phono preamplifier, Ortofon OM5e MM cartridge), Denon DP-300F automatic, Fluance RT85 (with Ortofon 2M Blue cartridge), Sony PS-LX310BT, the Audio-Technica AT-LP5x USB (premounted AT-VM95E cartridge, USB output), and the Crosley C100, which closely resembles a classic Technics SL-1200.

Tables with more robust plinths, better cartridges, more refined tonearms, and heavier platters include Pro-Ject's Debut Carbon EVO (includes Sumiko Rainier Phono cartridge), Clearaudio Concept, Technics SL-1500C, or the gorgeous Marantz TT-15S1 Reference Series (with Virtuoso MM cart).

If all-in-one players with included amplification and speakers are your desire, consider the following: The "1 by ONE High Fidelity, Belt-Drive Turntable with Built-in Speakers, Vinyl Record Player with Magnetic Cartridge, Bluetooth Playback and Aux-in Functionality, and Auto Off" is available at Amazon. Crosley sells a full system for less than the cost of a plane ticket between New York City and Washington, D.C., with turntable, powered speakers, and Bluetooth streaming. Similarly priced, House of Marley offers a smart-looking package that includes the House of Marley Stir It Up Wireless Turntable, Bluetooth, and built-in phono preamp—you need only add a speaker. The highly awarded Andover-One Turntable Music System

REMARKABLE **RECORD STORES**

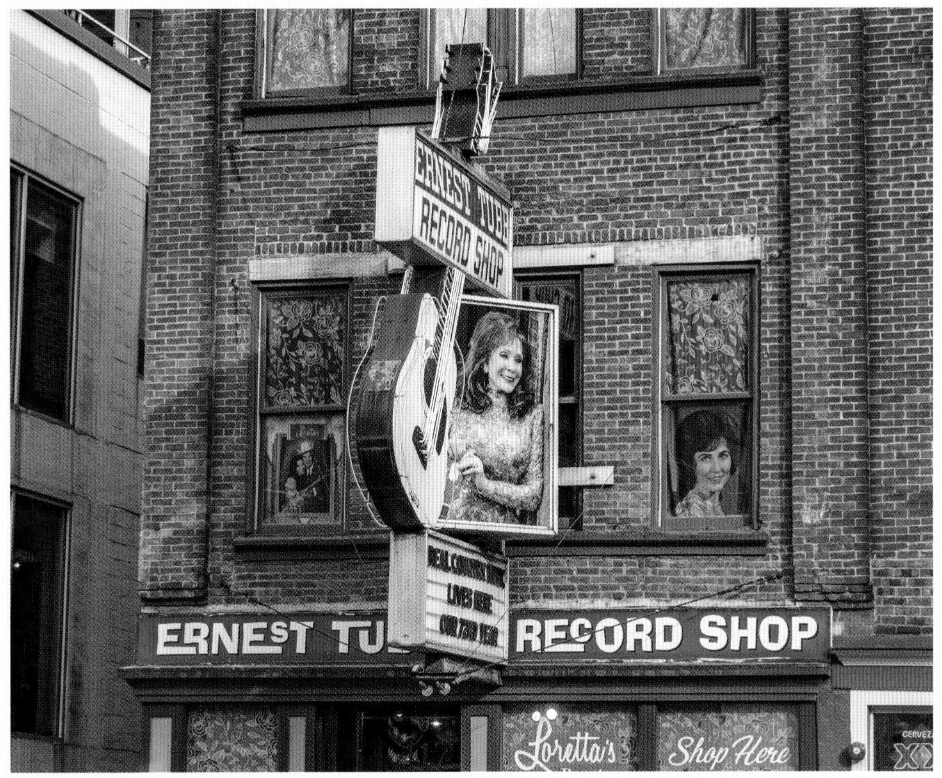

ERNEST TUBB RECORD SHOP • *NASHVILLE, TENNESSEE*

"Real country music lives here." When country star Ernest Tubb heard from too many fans how much difficulty they had in tracking down his records, he decided to open a country music store of his own in 1947. The shop also became renowned for its Saturday-night *Midnite Jamboree* broadcasts, held after the Grand Ole Opry broadcasts from the Ryman Auditorium just up the street on the same night. The store closed in 2022, though at the time of writing there were hopes it could be reopened. –*G.G.*

MP3

Basically a highly compressed digital audio file, the MP3 became ubiquitous for its downloadable ease and tiny file size, making it a natural for streaming on personal devices from such services as Spotify and Apple Music. Like the Walkman before it, Apple's iPod music player brought another wave of personal/portable audio to the fore, able to hold thousands of MP3s on its small internal hard drive. Though higher quality AIFF and FLAC files hold the complete digital information of the original master recording, the MP3 file is comparatively smaller and sonically inferior, which didn't stop it from becoming the standard for digital music playback on portable media players for fans of artists as diverse as Taylor Swift to Metallica and beyond. While CDs offered 16-bit depth/44.1kHz sample rate, high-res files can reach to 24/192 beyond CD's redbook resolution of 16/44, offering better sound from larger files. Whether a CD sounds better than a high-res file depends on the provenance of the MP3 file and the CD player used.

In the late 1990s, mp3.com offered free downloads of thousands of MP3s by independent artists. The MP3's tiny files created "peer-to-peer" sharing of music ripped from CDs, which gave birth to Napster, which benefitted from massive file sharing, resulting in rampant copyright infringement. Major record labels dubbed the practice "music piracy," and consequently sued Napster, eventually shutting down the site. But the damage was done; then and now, many consumers believe music should essentially be free, many streaming services offering MP3s of popular music free of charge, with advertisements. *–K.M.*

includes streaming, turntable with Pro-Ject tonearm, Ortofon 2M Silver cartridge, remote, and a six-speaker, Class-D powered "internal audio system."

Turntable Lab offers a complete system with Audio-Technica AT-LP60X turntable and powered Edifier R1280DB speakers; another package includes the Pro-Ject T1 Phono SB, Ortofon OM5e cart, and Sonos Five speaker with streaming technology.

The French-made La Boite Concept LX All-in-One Acoustic Loudspeaker brings console luxury to the party; a sleek, contemporary design with linen speaker grilles; and gold plated, retro-looking controls. Similarly, hand-built in San Diego, California, using "the finest American hardwoods and carefully selected materials," Wrensilva offers very expensive, exquisitely made turntable-based consoles including VPI turntables and tonearms, Ortofon cartridges, chunky 1950s-looking control dials, and Class-D amplification by ICEpower/Bang & Olufsen.

If top-tier sound, the best designs, and materials matter—cost no object—consider the Kuzma Stabi R with 4Point turntable, VPI Avenger Direct with 3D Fatboy Gimbal tonearm, Acoustic Signature Montana NEO, Clearaudio Reference Jubilee, Döhmann Audio Helix One Mk2, or Thorens TD 124 DD.

Similarly cartridges are available at *every* price point. Quality entry-level carts include the classic Denon DL-103 MC, Goldring E3, Audio-Technica AT-VM95C, and Ortofon 2M Blue and Red. Mid-price carts which begin to stress the wallet include the Ortofon 2M Black, Sumiko Wellfleet, and Sumiko Songbird. Truly over-the-top, best-in-the-world-status carts include the Tzar DST, Miyajima Labs Madake Snakewood, Lyra Atlas SL λ Lambda, and Air Tight PC-1 Coda, each of which will set you back the cost of a well-cared-for, low-mileage used car. ◊

SOMETHING UP THE SLEEVE

THE ART OF THE LP

BY MARTIN POPOFF

↑ Beginning his career at the American Gramophone Company, Alex Steinweiss might be considered the father of sleeve design. By the late 1930s he was designing jackets for 78rpm records every bit as sophisticated as jazz covers we'd see in the 1950s.

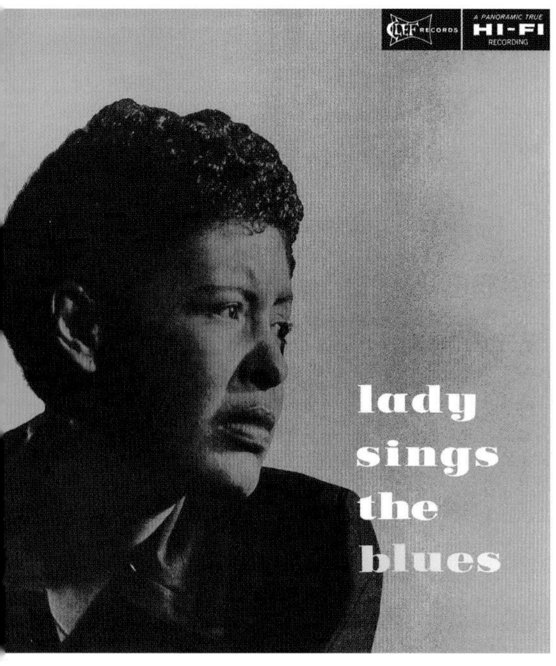

Overlaying the history of album cover design with the invention of the 33⅓ LP is a bit of a mug's game unless one tries to pin down the moving parts. Fortunately there's one name we can conjure to make sense of the trajectory, and that would be Alex Steinweiss. Beginning his career at the American Gramophone Company (soon to be Columbia) at the age of 22, Steinweiss was off to the races designing jackets for 78rpm records that were every bit as graphically sophisticated as the celebrated jazz covers we'd see in the 1950s. But there are three additional dates to consider. His first design was in 1938, with more iconic sleeves added through the 1940s. This is followed by the invention of the 33⅓rpm record in June 1948, with the first marketed product showing up in Columbia's 1949 catalog—Alex's previously used Greek column motif adorned the first record using the new technology. By 1953, in collaboration with the Imperial Paper Box, Steinweiss had invented the box construction that would be in use, with variation, until the CD age and beyond.

By the early 1950s we'd already seen a sort of "golden age" of album design (applied primarily to classical albums, soundtracks, and most freshly jazz records), but the medium was mostly collage-minded illustration with a limited color palette, spiced with inventive type—modern art without the use of actual modern art. The 1953 design (paper printed using a four-color CMYK [cyan, magenta, yellow, key/black] process and glued to

← Three of the most widely celebrated early jackets circa 1953 to 1959 were Gene Vincent and His Blue Caps' *Bluejean Bop!*, Billie Holiday's *Lady Sings the Blues*, and Little Richard's *Here's Little Richard* (right page). Like other notable contemporaries, all incorporated photography augmented by stylized coloring and deft typestyle selection and text placement.

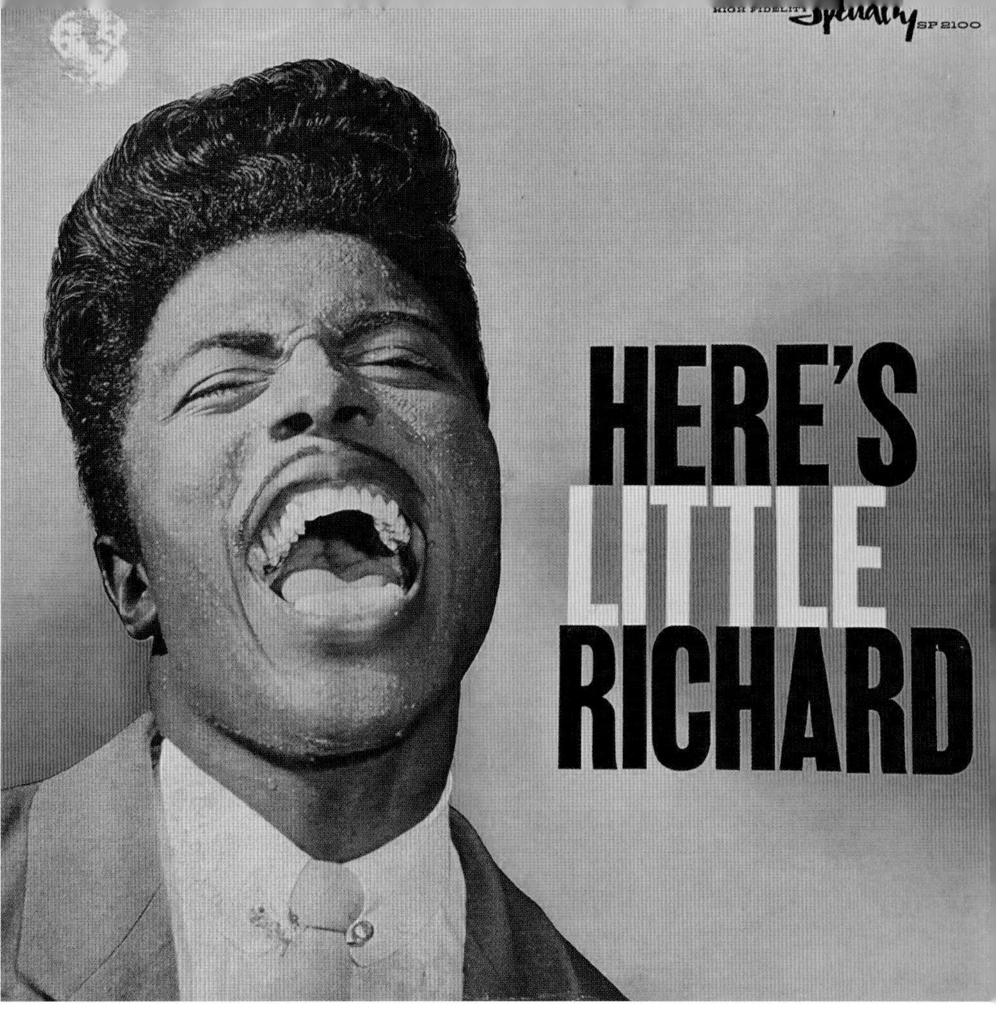

a cardboard housing) allowed for the use of photography, yet another innovation we can assign to Steinweiss.

Back to the mug's game, proclaiming greatest album covers is full on a matter of opinion. But some of the most widely celebrated early jackets circa 1953 to 1959 (made all the more iconic due to the high regard for the music enclosed) would include Chuck Berry's *Berry Is on Top*, Johnny Cash's *Johnny Cash with His Hot and Blue Guitar!*, *Ray Charles*, John Coltrane's *Blue Train*, *Bo Diddley*, *The Fabulous Wailers*, Billie Holiday's *Lady Sings the Blues*, *Buddy Holly*, Little Richard's *Here's Little Richard*, Elvis Presley's self-titled *Elvis*, Nina Simone's *Little Girl Blue*, Gene Vincent and His Blue Caps' *Bluejean Bop!*, Sonny Boy Williamson's *Down and Out Blues*, and Tito Puente and His Orchestra's *Dance Mania*. All feature photography augmented, in most cases, by stylized additional coloring and deft typestyle selection and text placement. Still, looking back—even from a vantage point as long ago as the late 1960s—there's a sense that the potential of cover design had barely been tapped.

← Four lads from Liverpool show off the gatefold of their new LP, *Sgt. Pepper's Lonely Hearts Club Band*. On occasion, the gatefold became as iconic as the outer sleeve itself.

GATEFOLDS

It might not seem like much, but gatefold sleeves doubled the surface of the album cover, allowing for some iconic inner spreads that became as famed as the album covers themselves, with Kiss's *Alive II* and Black Sabbath's *We Sold Our Soul for Rock 'n' Roll* being two examples. But gatefolds have been around since the "photo album" presentation of records, with the first one of the 33⅓ era cited as *Ella Fitzgerald Sings the Cole Porter Songbook*. It's a double album, one record in each gusseted sleeve, which is the reason for gatefolds in the first place (although many gatefolds throughout history have housed single albums). The inner gate of the Ella Fitzgerald album offers another early innovation, namely the idea of extensive liner notes, which fill the inner two panels and spill over onto the back.

In the rock realm, early gates include records by Elvis Presley (multiple titles), Fabian (again, liner notes and photos), and the Everly Brothers, whose *A Date With* album uses the gatefold to try sell us on joining the fan club. The next milestones in gatefold use would arrive circa 1964 with *The Beatles Story* and then *Help!* the following year. Then there's The Mothers of Invention's *Freak Out!*, a record also considered the first concept album; The Rolling Stones' *Big Hits (High Tide and Green Grass)*; and Bob Dylan's *Blonde on Blonde*, all from 1966.

Gatefold covers also offered the opportunity to present a continuous work of art from the front cover wrapping around the spine to the back. We see this with Miles Davis's *Bitches Brew*, David Bowie's *Aladdin Sane*, Elton John's *Captain Fantastic and the Brown Dirt Cowboy*, Led Zeppelin's *Houses of the Holy*, Boston's *Don't Look Back*, and a record considered the ultimate in prog-rock excess, *Tales from Topographic Oceans* by Yes, which allows celebrated illustrator Roger Dean to go wild. Ted Nugent's *Cat Scratch Fever*, Peter Frampton's *Frampton Comes Alive!*, and *Honey* from the Ohio Players offer examples of continuous gatefold shots that read vertically—portrait mode versus landscape, as it were.

For excess in this department, there are triple gates like *Tommy* from The Who and *All the World's a Stage* from Rush, as well as gates with extra booklets stitched in like *Uriah Heep Live* and *Black Sabbath Vol 4*. But the winner's got to be *Space Ritual* from Hawkwind, which comes housed in a Barney Bubbles–designed sleeve that unfolds to reveal a flat cardboard sheet of six panels per side.

In the modern era, many reissues of non-gatefold albums are now in newly designed gated sleeves due to there being an additional one or even two vinyl records stuffed with bonus tracks, demos, and/or live shows. This space is often used for the printing of lyrics that were not included the first time out or new retrospective essays (of which this author has penned more than a few for this very purpose!). As well, most vinyl reissues of CD-era albums need at least two pieces of vinyl to contain the longer running order of most CDs, again, facilitating a gate.

ICONIC **COVERS**

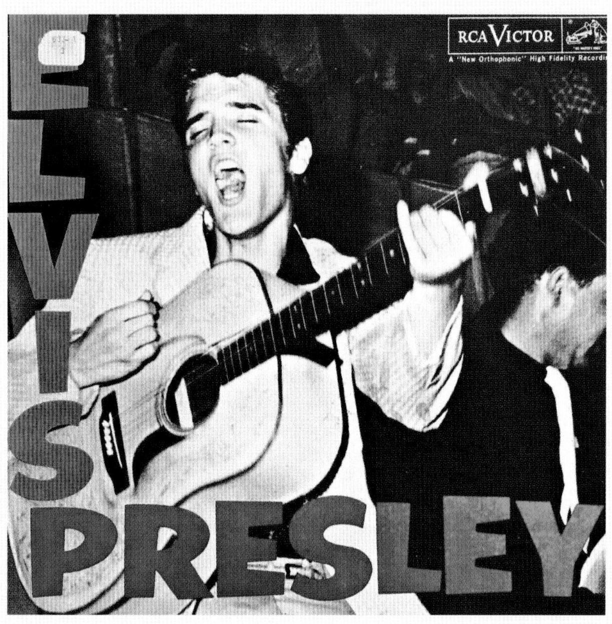

ELVIS PRESLEY

ELVIS PRESLEY

Important also because it's the very first Elvis album (and thus one of the first rock 'n' roll full-lengths), this cover is iconic due to its blaring text and early use of photography, in this case William "Red" Robertson's shot underscoring the mania about to kick off. Reimagined in later years for The Clash's *London Calling*. –M.P.

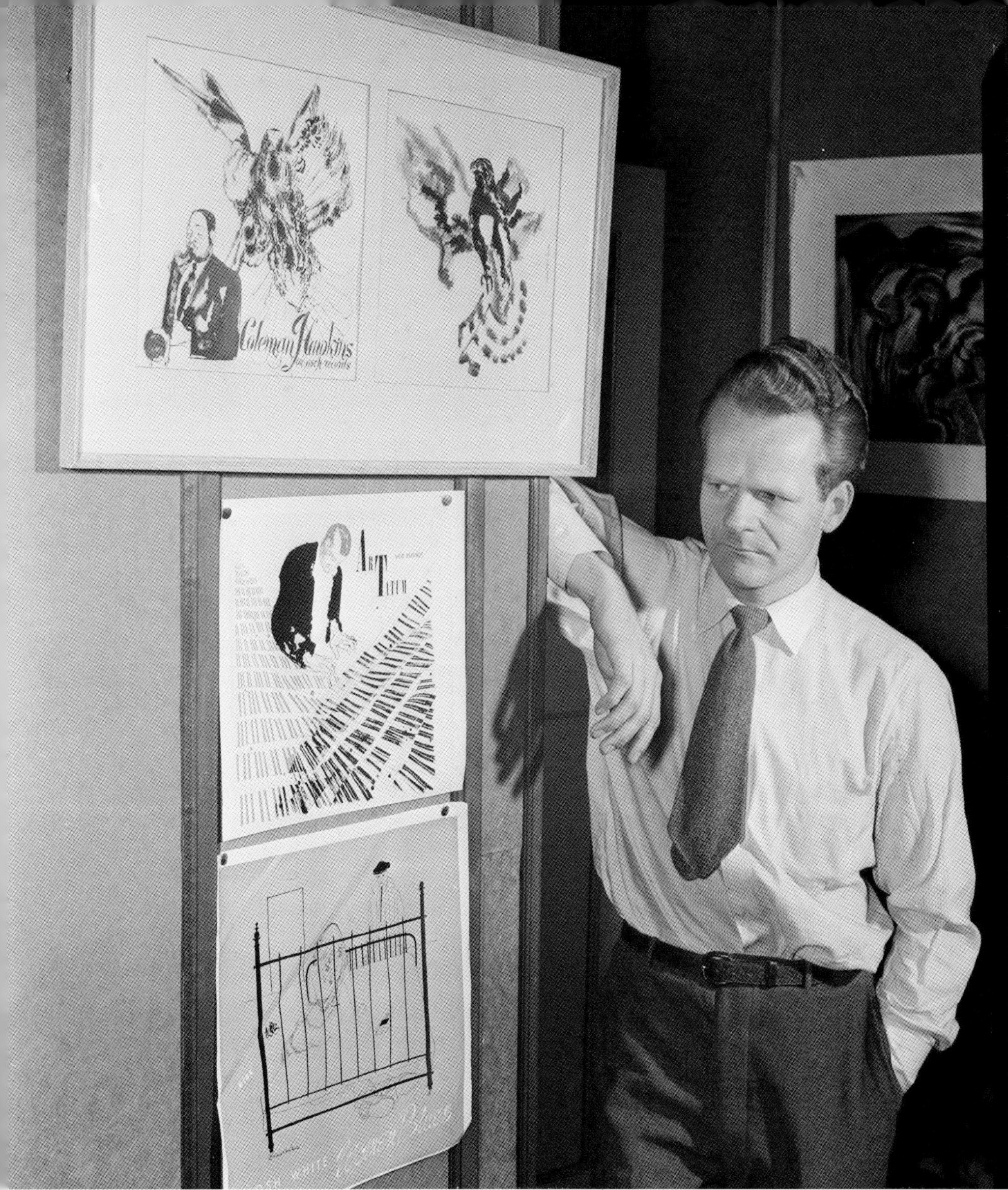

← In the 1950s and 1960s, labels had regularly utilized illustrators. Notable was David Stone Martin, who worked in color but is most renowned for his line drawings of jazz greats using black ink.

ILLUSTRATION

In the 1950s and 1960s, labels had regularly utilized illustrators, designers, and photographers; but their personal imprint was usually subtle. Notable was the team of photographer Francis Wolff and designer Reid Miles, who together created the Blue Note Records jazz aesthetic, as well as David Stone Martin, who worked in color but is most renowned for his line drawings of jazz greats using black ink. It wasn't until the 1970s that we started to see both design houses and lone-gun illustrators with identifiable styles and languages.

REMARKABLE **RECORD STORES**

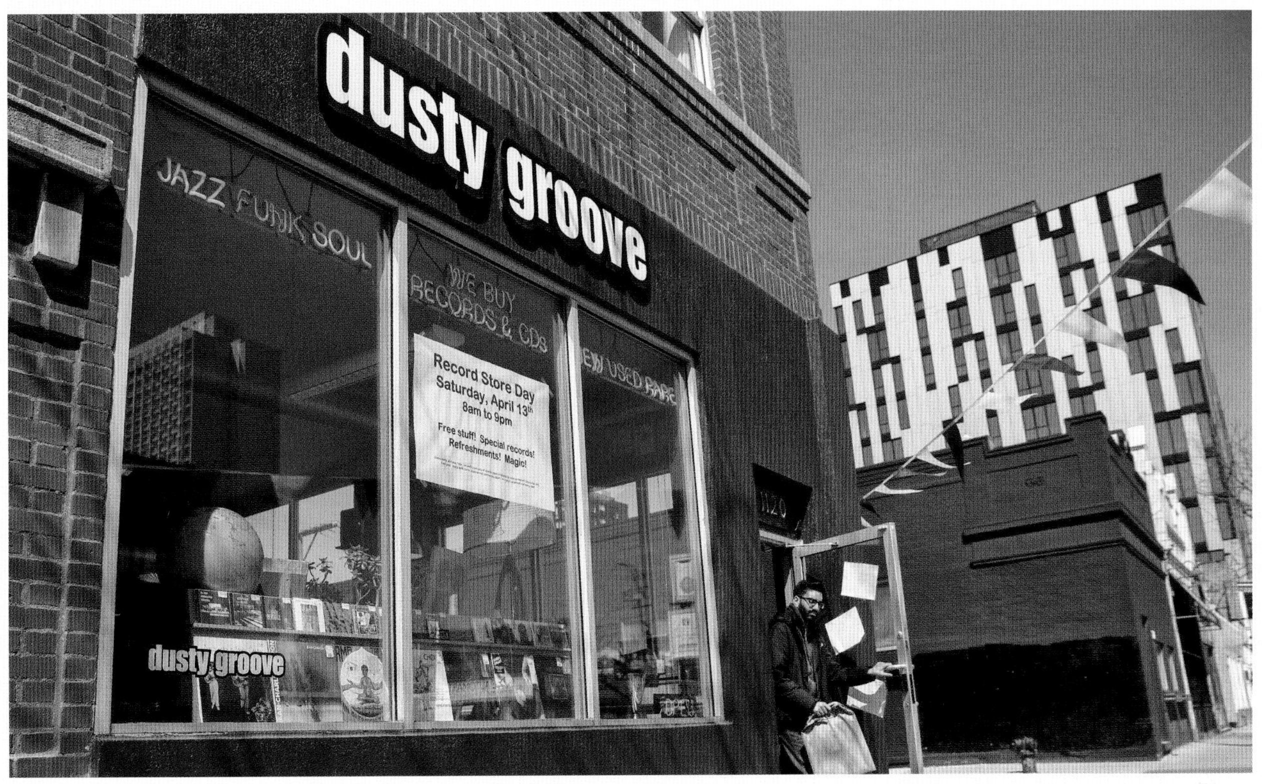

DUSTY GROOVE • *CHICAGO, ILLINOIS*

In a reversal of the usual process, Dusty Groove opened as an online-only retailer in August 1996. But demand led to in-person sales by the end of the year, and by the end of 2001, their physical store was open seven days a week. Though the store started out as vinyl only, it eventually expanded to carrying CDs, not to mention the wealth of cheap offerings to be found in the store's Bargain Basement. There's an affiliated label, Dusty Groove America (the shop's original name), and a documentary, *Dusty Groove: The Sound of Transition*. –G.G.

← Roger Dean was prominent in the sleeve illustration camp, creating planetary climates in which fans could lose themselves, particularly for prog-rock band Yes.

In the illustration camp, of most prominence was Roger Dean, who dabbled in Uriah Heep but then really threw his lot in with Yes, creating delicious and colorful planetary climates where the fans could lose themselves as they pondered what five spiritual traditions Jon Anderson was drawing from at once.

Predating Roger Dean were the artists first associated with psychedelic poster art, most notably Stanley "Mouse" Miller, who started out illustrating hot rods on T-shirts in the "monster" style associated with Ed "Big Daddy" Roth. He created the skull and roses motif for The Grateful Dead along with covers for them

↑ Stanley "Mouse" Miller, who started out illustrating "monster" hot rods, created the skull and roses motif for The Grateful Dead.

and offshoot projects. The Steve Miller Band and Journey also benefited brand-wise from his sumptuous, upscale, jewel-like illustrations and attention to type.

Ken Kelly was epic in a more symbolist manner, doing Rainbow's *Rising*, Kiss's *Destroyer* and *Love Gun*, en route to Manowar. Speaking of mighty heavy metal, Iron Maiden enlisted the services of Derek Riggs, who showed Rod Smallwood and Steve Harris a preexisting green monster he'd done. "Eddie" was born and would become one of the most lucrative and marketable band mascots in history, really, a crucial factor in Iron

LEGENDARY **LABELS**

ELEKTRA

From the early 1950s through the late 1960s, Elektra might have been the most interesting indie label. Although most known for folk music and one of the folk revival's biggest stars, Judy Collins, it also developed a respected classical music catalog on its Nonesuch subsidiary. It then helped spark the burgeoning market for rock LPs in the mid- to late 1960s with the Paul Butterfield Blues Band, Love, and especially The Doors. Elektra releases were distinguished by meticulous attention to recording quality and imaginative and, at times, idiosyncratic artwork overseen by Bill Harvey. While The Doors had its biggest and best hits, Elektra continued to record adventurous cult rock artists like Tim Buckley, The MC5, The Stooges, The Incredible String Band, and Nico, losing much of its personality when it was absorbed into Warner Communications and chief Jac Holzman left the company in the early 1970s. *–R.U.*

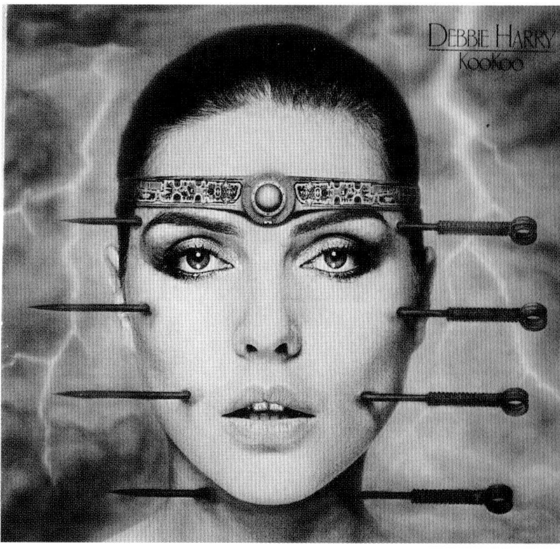

Maiden's success. Also in the mascot department is Motörhead's "Snaggletooth," created by another prolific album cover illustrator, Joe Petagno. More ghoulish than any of the many versions of Riggs's Eddie is the oeuvre of Swiss artistic polymath H. R. Giger, whose nightmarish "biomechanical" vision can be seen on covers for Emerson, Lake & Palmer; Danzig; Debbie Harry; and Celtic Frost.

↑ Swiss artist H. R. Giger at work in his Zürich studio (left). His "biomechanical" vision is seen here on a Debbie Harry cover (top).

↑ Designed for British heavy metal act Iron Maiden, Derek Riggs's "Eddie" became one of the most lucrative mascots in rock history (bottom).

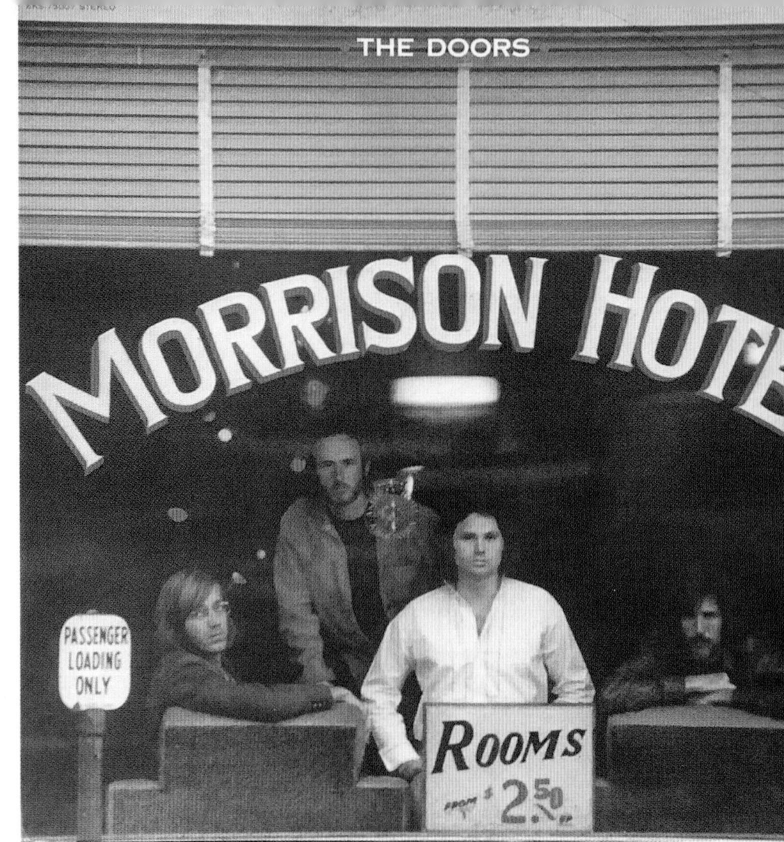

↑ Capturing the earthy vibe of Laurel Canyon, Henry Diltz shot over 200 album covers, most famously Morrison Hotel from The Doors and the self-titled release from Crosby, Stills & Nash.

PHOTOGRAPHY

We've talked about yummy paintings, but what about the great photographers who near single-handedly created some of the industry's greatest sleeves? Back at the advent of photography on covers, there was the aforementioned Blue Note's Francis Wolff, who worked with John Coltrane, Art Blakey, Hank Mobley, Miles Davis, and Wayne Shorter. Lee Friedlander worked with Coltrane as well, plus Charles Mingus, Ray Charles, and dozens more. Phil "Snapdragon" Stern, notable more so for documenting Hollywood film stars, had a simple headshot style that can be seen on dozens of landmark jazz albums issued by Verve Records.

Notable in the rock era, it was Iain Macmillan who shot the conspiratorial image used for the cover of The Beatles' *Abbey Road*, in consultation with Paul McCartney and Apple in-house designer Kosh. Macmillan would go on to work with John Lennon and Yoko Ono primarily. Henry Diltz shot over 200 covers, including records for The Hollies, Mama Cass, Arlo Guthrie, Steppenwolf, The Lovin' Spoonful, and most famously *Morrison Hotel* from The Doors and the self-titled release from Crosby, Stills & Nash. His plain style captured the dusty earthiness of the Laurel Canyon "avocado mafia" scene perfectly. Jerry Schatzberg was another prominent figure who worked on dozens of sleeves, shooting the likes of Bob Dylan, The Rolling Stones, and Aretha Franklin.

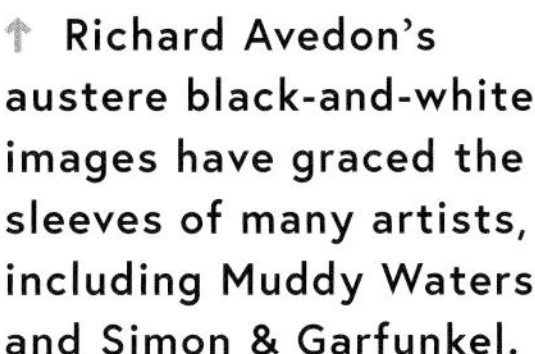

↑ Richard Avedon's austere black-and-white images have graced the sleeves of many artists, including Muddy Waters and Simon & Garfunkel.

Photographers known more for fashion but nonetheless impacted the medium at hand include Jean-Paul Goude, who did many sharp, angular covers for Grace Jones, including the stark and memorable *Island Life*; Jean-Baptiste Mondino, who shot a naked Prince for the cover of *Lovesexy* (but mostly does videos); and *Vogue* magazine's Richard Avedon, who has captured austere black-and-white images of Sly and the Family Stone, Barbra Streisand, Joan Baez, Muddy Waters, Sparks, Cher, and Bob Weir. It was Helmut Newton, also known for his work with *Vogue*, who shot the cover image for the Scorpions' *Love at First Sting* and a

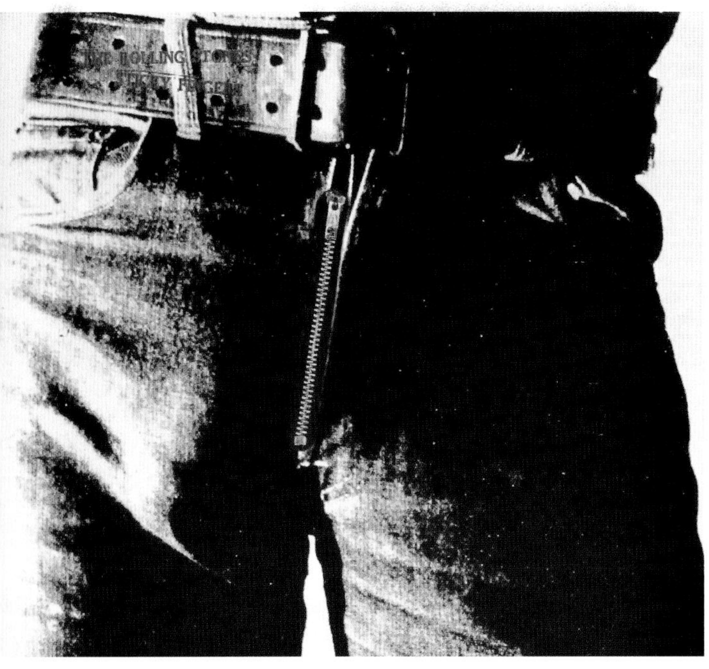

handful of sleeves for Missing Persons and Visage, all in black and white. He also did Van Halen's *Women and Children First*, along with the album's six-panel poster portraying a bare-chested David Lee Roth chained to a fence. Finally, also from the Vogue camp, is Steven Meisel, who worked with Andy Fraser from Free, Rod Stewart, and Whitney Houston but is most known for his work on the cover of Madonna's *Like a Virgin*.

Andy Warhol represents a mix of photography and, more than anything, a distinctly pastel approach to color. But some of his sleeves that make use of portraiture include albums for Aretha Franklin, John Lennon, Paul Anka, Diana Ross, Billy Squier, and The Rolling Stones. What's also interesting about Warhol is that he was there for the early days of illustrated covers, creating his first sleeve in 1949 at the age of 21. And who can forget Mick Rock, who's created some of the most iconic front covers of all time for the likes of Queen, Iggy & the Stooges, Lou Reed, and David Bowie?

It's all in the name of marketing. First off, the more famed the photographer, potentially the more iconic and recognizable the final image. As well, the recording artist gets bragging rights, inclined to bring up in interviews the photo session as some sort of marker that their band has "arrived" (I speak from experience!).

← **Andy Warhol's most famous sleeves are arguably those he created for The Velvet Underground and The Rolling Stones (pictured), but he actually created his first sleeve in 1949, a collection of Mexican music for the Columbia label.**

ICONIC **COVERS**

THE VELVET UNDERGROUND & NICO • THE VELVET UNDERGROUND & NICO

Maybe the most outrageous cover as of early 1967, what we've got here is an album upon which the designer's name is prominently placed along with the words "Peel slowly and see" and nothing indicative of the band. Peeling back the sticker on the pictured banana reveals a two-tone flesh-colored banana underneath. *–M.P.*

DESIGNER AS GENERALIST

Typically it takes a manager of sorts, an organizer—often working at the record company, but not always—to commission visual artists and photographers and then worry about text placement and additional graphic elements.

Barney Bubbles was one of these jacks-of-all-trades, establishing himself with Hawkwind but then diving headlong into English punk and new wave, creating clean, geometric sleeves for The Damned, Ian Dury, and the rest of the pub rock gang, namely Nick Lowe, Dave Edmunds, and Elvis Costello. More austere but

↑ British rock group The Who with artist Peter Blake. Forever linked to the *Sgt. Pepper's Lonely Hearts Club Band* cover, Blake also designed the cover for The Who's *Face Dances*.

in the same wheelhouse was Manchester's Peter Saville, who came up with the trademark clinical look of Factory Records, the label he cofounded with Tony Erasmus and Tony Wilson. His designs for the likes of Orchestral Manoeuvres in the Dark, Roxy Music, King Crimson, Joy Division, and, most prolifically, New Order established an aesthetic that influenced the look of many covers in the 1980s, especially at the synth-pop end of the market. His mark can also be seen in the aesthetic created by Vaughan Oliver at label 4AD, most notably for the Pixies. Also in this camp is Malcolm Garrett, whose generally futuristic collage style was applied to covers for the Buzzcocks, Magazine, Heaven 17, Duran Duran, and Simple Minds.

Also notable as a pure designer is Peter Blake, forever linked to the *Sgt. Pepper's Lonely Hearts Club Band* cover, but also having worked with Ian Dury, Eric Clapton, George Harrison, and Pentangle. For The Who's *Face Dances* record of 1981, he commissioned famous artists (including David Hockney) to paint individual portraits of the band members. Included with the album was a four-panel poster of the cover.

Then there are designers who worked as part of the label staff, like Roslav Szaybo and Paula Scher, both at CBS. Szaybo is famed for the update of Judas Priest's logo as well as the art for the *Stained Class* and *British Steel* albums. As art director at CBS Records, Scher is estimated to have designed more than 150 covers over an eight-year span. John Berg, at the associated Columbia in the United States, is said to have worked on more than 5,000 covers, commissioning both illustrators and photographers but leaning toward the latter, while also focusing on distinctive type selection and placement and favoring gatefolds. His marquee projects include *The Barbra Streisand Album*, *Bob Dylan's Greatest Hits*, and Bruce Springsteen's *Born to Run*. Also of note is Ed Thrasher, who worked for Warner Bros. and is known for his work on The Jimi Hendrix Experience's *Are You Experienced*, Van Morrison's *Astral Weeks*, Nancy Sinatra's *Nancy*, Curtis Mayfield's *There's No Place Like America Today*, Joni Mitchell's *Clouds*, and Funkadelic's *One Nation Under Groove*.

ICONIC **COVERS**

TIME OUT • THE DAVE BRUBECK QUARTET

Not only did Sadamitsu "S. Neil" Fujita art-direct approximately fifty album covers, being the first to commission works for Columbia; he occasionally used his own abstract canvases, as he did for this landmark jazz classic. Fujita's energetic painting nicely suggests the pop and sparkle of the music enclosed. He's also used the colors in the painting to help make sense of the complicated bank of text above it. Group with *Mingus Ah Um* (Charles Mingus) and *Modern Jazz Perspective* (Don Byrd and Gigi Gryce) and we've practically got a triptych. *–M.P.*

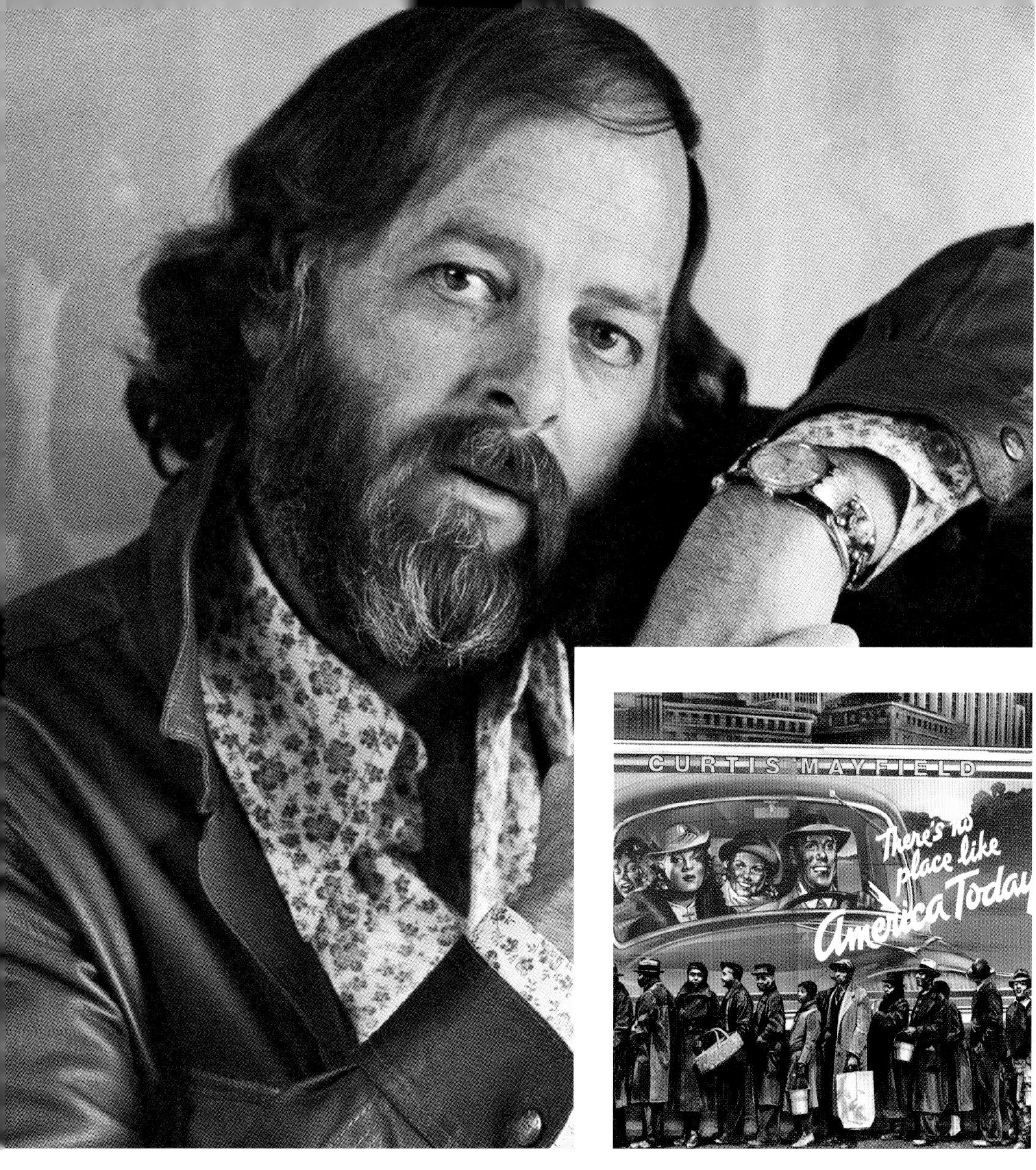

↑ Notable designer and photographer Ed Thrasher is known for his work on The Jimi Hendrix Experience's *Are You Experienced* and Nancy Sinatra's *Boots*, among others.

Bottom line, what we are talking about here generally falls under the job title of art director, who, as the industry developed through the 1970s and 1980s, could have a huge impact on the sales of any given record if its artwork struck a chord. Intrigue, shock factor, narrative, an underscoring of the music enclosed, or, indeed, amusing incongruity with the music enclosed . . . it's why they give out Grammy Awards for cover design. But as important as accolades and bragging rights might be up and down the halls of Atlantic or A&M, what usually mattered most was this: "Does it look good on a T-shirt?"

DESIGN HOUSES

To be sure, some design houses had a fancy name created and adopted by what was, in reality, a very small team (or even arguably, in some cases, a company of one); but they did indeed exist, with Hipgnosis and Pacific Eye & Ear being most prominent. Others contributing to the field included Album Graphics, Inc., who did The Supremes, Rod Stewart, *Fly by Night* for Rush, and both legendary New York Dolls covers. Because they were based in Chicago, much of their work was for Mercury, which was headquartered there in the 1970s. Then there was CCS Advertising, associated with early Island Records and some of the prog-adjacent bands in the United Kingdom in the early 1970s. Also from the United Kingdom was Cream, who were prolific well into the 1980s, taking over when Hipgnosis gave up the ghost.

Pacific Eye & Ear was the domain of one Ernie Cefalu, who worked with a team including Drew Struzan and Ingid Haenke on nearly 200 covers in the 1970s, including *Welcome to My Nightmare* and *Greatest Hits* for Alice Cooper, *Toys in the Attic* and *Rocks* for Aerosmith, and the incendiary occult ritual played out across both sides of Black Sabbath's *Sabbath Bloody Sabbath*.

← Commandeered by Aubrey Powell and Storm Thorgerson (pictured), Hipgnosis is the most storied album design house, their portfolio anchored by hugely celebrated Pink Floyd presentations such as *Animals*. →

But it is Hipgnosis, commandeered by Aubrey Powell and Storm Thorgerson, that is the most storied of the album cover design houses. Beginning as quick replacement designers for Pink Floyd, Powell and Thorgerson went on to a career anchored by hugely celebrated Floyd presentations, while also working with the likes of Led Zeppelin, Bad Company, UFO, 10cc, Genesis, Black Sabbath, Wishbone Ash, Styx, and Peter Gabriel. Hipgnosis made the careers of designers like George Hardie, Richard Evans, and Richard Manning, who were all part of the company's complex and yet identifiable style, one that made surreal use of collaged trick photography, photo tinting, geometric elements, and custom-designed lettering. Deluxe packaging was also part and parcel of the company's designs, particularly contributing to the perceived specialness of Pink Floyd. Once the company dissolved in 1983, Thorgerson continued as a solo artist with a slightly adjusted vision, in which sculpture and contemporary artworks were inserted into his still-surreal landscapes.

All told, the influence of Hipgnosis can't be overstated. Although it can't be said that their visual language lived on particularly, they raised the game of all the designers around them in the mid- to late 1970s and then neatly stepped aside for a new wave to take over in the 1980s. In other words, Hipgnosis were inspirers, exemplars of how album cover art can be serious art. In that sense, they were The Beatles of the genre.

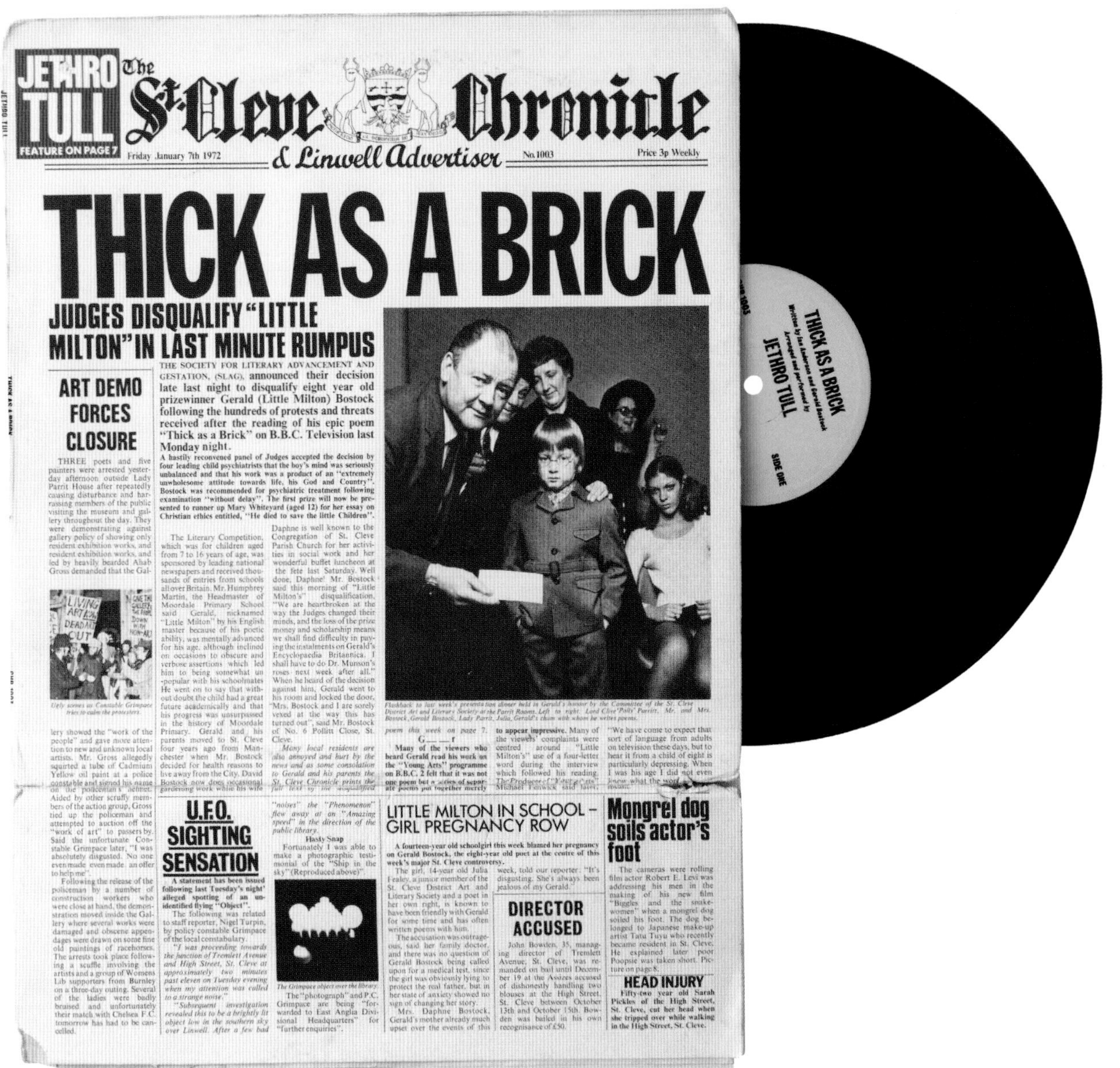

JETHRO TULL FEATURE ON PAGE 7

The St. Cleve Chronicle & Linwell Advertiser

Friday January 7th 1972 — No.1003 — Price 3p Weekly

THICK AS A BRICK

JUDGES DISQUALIFY "LITTLE MILTON" IN LAST MINUTE RUMPUS

THE SOCIETY FOR LITERARY ADVANCEMENT AND GESTATION, (SLAG), **announced their decision late last night to disqualify eight year old prizewinner Gerald (Little Milton) Bostock following the hundreds of protests and threats received after the reading of his epic poem "Thick as a Brick" on B.B.C. Television last Monday night.**

A hastily reconvened panel of Judges accepted the decision by four leading child psychiatrists that the boy's mind was seriously unbalanced and that his work was a product of an "extremely unwholesome attitude towards life, his God and Country". Bostock was recommended for psychiatric treatment following examination "without delay". The first prize will now be presented to runner up Mary Whiteyard (aged 12) for her essay on Christian ethics entitled, "He died to save the little Children".

The Literary Competition, which was for children aged from 7 to 16 years of age, was sponsored by leading national newspapers and received thousands of entries from schools all over Britain. Mr. Humphrey Martin, the Headmaster of Moordale Primary School said Gerald, nicknamed "Little Milton" by his English master because of his poetic ability, was mentally advanced for his age, although inclined on occasions to obscure and verbose assertions which led him to being somewhat un-popular with his schoolmates He went on to say that without doubt the child had a great future academically and that his progress was unsurpassed in the history of Moordale Primary. Gerald and his parents moved to St. Cleve four years ago from Manchester when Mr. Bostock decided for health reasons to live away from the City. David Bostock now does occasional gardening work while his wife Daphne is well known to the Congregation of St. Cleve Parish Church for her activities in social work and her wonderful buffet luncheon at the fete last Saturday. Well done, Daphne! Mr. Bostock said this morning of "Little Milton's" disqualification, "We are heartbroken at the way the Judges changed their minds, and the loss of the prize money and scholarship means we shall find difficulty in paying the instalments on Gerald's Encyclopaedia Britannica. I shall have to do Dr. Munson's roses next week after all." When he heard of the decision against him, Gerald went to his room and locked the door. "Mrs. Bostock and I are sorely vexed at the way this has turned out", said Mr. Bostock of No. 6 Pollitt Close, St. Cleve.

Many local residents are also annoyed and hurt by the news and as some consolation to Gerald and his parents the St. Cleve Chronicle prints the full text of the disqualified poem this week on page 7.

G— —r

Many of the viewers who heard Gerald read his work on the "Young Arts" programme on B.B.C. 2 felt that it was not one poem but a series of separate poems put together merely to appear impressive. Many of the viewers' complaints were centred around "Little Milton's" use of a four-letter word during the interview which followed his reading. The Producer of "Young Arts" Michael Fenwick said later, "We have come to expect that sort of language from adults on television these days, but to hear it from a child of eight is particularly depressing. When I was his age I did not even know what the word [illegible] meant."

Flashback to last week's presentation dinner held in Gerald's honour by the Committee of the St. Cleve District Art and Literary Society at the Parrit Rooms. Left to right: Lord Clive 'Polly' Parrit, Mr. and Mrs. Bostock, Gerald Bostock, Lady Parrit, Julia, Gerald's chum with whom he writes poems.

ART DEMO FORCES CLOSURE

THREE poets and five painters were arrested yesterday afternoon outside Lady Parrit House after repeatedly causing disturbance and harrassing members of the public visiting the museum and gallery throughout the day. They were demonstrating against gallery policy of showing only resident exhibition works, and resident exhibition works, and led by heavily bearded Ahab Gross demanded that the Gallery showed the "work of the people" and gave more attention to new and unknown local artists. Mr. Gross allegedly squirted a tube of Cadmium Yellow oil paint at a police constable and signed his name on the policeman's helmet. Aided by other scruffy members of the action group, Gross tied up the policeman and attempted to auction off the "work of art" to passers by. Said the unfortunate Constable Grimpace later, "I was absolutely disgusted. No one even made even made an offer to help me".

Following the release of the policeman by a number of construction workers who were close at hand, the demonstration moved inside the Gallery where several works were damaged and obscene appendages were drawn on some fine old paintings of racehorses. The arrests took place following a scuffle involving the artists and a group of Womens Lib supporters from Burnley on a three-day outing. Several of the ladies were badly bruised and unfortunately their match with Chelsea F.C. tomorrow has had to be cancelled.

Ugly scenes as Constable Grimpace tries to calm the protesters.

U.F.O. SIGHTING SENSATION

A statement has been issued following last Tuesday's night' alleged spotting of an unidentified flying "Object".

The following was related to staff reporter, Nigel Turpin, by policy constable Grimpace of the local constabulary.

"I was proceeding towards the junction of Tremlett Avenue and High Street, St. Cleve at approximately two minutes past eleven on Tuesday evening when my attention was called to a strange noise."

"Subsequent investigation revealed this to be a brightly lit object low in the southern sky over Linwell. After a few bad "noises" the "Phenomenon" flew away at an "Amazing speed" in the direction of the public library.

Hasty Snap

Fortunately I was able to make a photographic testimonial of the "Ship in the sky" (Reproduced above)".

The Grimpace object over the library.

The "photograph" and P.C. Grimpace are being "forwarded to East Anglia Divisional Headquarters" for "further enquiries".

LITTLE MILTON IN SCHOOL – GIRL PREGNANCY ROW

A fourteen-year old schoolgirl this week blamed her pregnancy on Gerald Bostock, the eight-year old poet at the centre of this week's major St. Cleve controversy.

The girl, 14-year old Julia Fealey, a junior member of the St. Cleve District Art and Literary Society and a poet in her own right, is known to have been friendly with Gerald for some time and has often written poems with him.

The accusation was outrageous, said her family doctor, and there was no question of Gerald Bostock being called upon for a medical test, since the girl was obviously lying to protect the real father, but in her state of anxiety showed no sign of changing her story.

Mrs. Daphne Bostock, Gerald's mother already much upset over the events of this week, told our reporter: "It's disgusting. She's always been jealous of my Gerald."

DIRECTOR ACCUSED

John Bowden, 35, managing director of Tremlett Avenue, St. Cleve, was remanded on bail until December 19 at the Assizes accused of dishonestly handling two blouses at the High Street, St. Cleve between October 13th and October 15th. Bowden was bailed in his own recognisance of £50.

Mongrel dog soils actor's foot

The cameras were rolling film actor Robert E. Levi was addressing his men in the making of his new film "Biggles and the snake-women" when a mongrel dog soiled his foot. The dog belonged to Japanese make-up artist Tatu Tuyu who recently became resident in St. Cleve. He explained later poor Poopsie was taken short. Picture on page 8.

HEAD INJURY

Fifty-two year old Sarah Pickles of the High Street, St. Cleve, cut her head when she tripped over while walking in the High Street, St. Cleve.

↑ **The fake newspaper included in their album *Thick as a Brick* made prog rockers Jethro Tull early adopters of novelty packaging.**

NOVELTY PACKAGING

As printing technology improved and rock became big business after the advent of the PA system and the first massive festivals, labels were looking for a leg up on the competition. As in many departments, The Beatles were in on the ground floor with inserted booklets and posters back in the late 1960s—the self-titled "White Album" featured blind embossing, numbering, a gatefold sleeve, a poster, and four individual portrait prints. We also started to see stickers included, plus the use of foil and die-cuts, one elaborate example of the latter being Jethro Tull's *Stand Up*, where a pop-up version of the band appeared when one opened the gate (their *Thick as a Brick* album included a fake newspaper). Also on the die-cut front, both Led

REMARKABLE **RECORD STORES**

THE SUB POP AIRPORT STORE • SEATAC, WASHINGTON

One of the few record stores located inside an airport (Seattle-Tacoma International), the only way you can patronize the store is by clearing the TSA security checkpoints. There's plenty of vinyl, listening stations, Sub Pop–themed merchandise (clothing, mugs, coffee), and books about (or written by) Sub Pop bands. Throw in the occasional in-store performance, and it's a fine place to pass the time while waiting for your next flight. –*G.G.*

LEGENDARY **LABELS**

STAX

Motown's main competitor for soul supremacy, the Memphis-based Stax label never seriously rivaled the Detroit company for sheer quantities of records sold. But from the early 1960s to the mid-1970s, no other outfit recorded as much prime Southern soul. Otis Redding, Booker T. & the MG's, Rufus Thomas, and his daughter Carla Thomas were the biggest Stax stars in its early years, the discs sometimes coming out on its sister label, Volt. Stax overcame Redding's death in late 1967, and the takeover of its catalog shortly afterward by Atlantic to remain a soul powerhouse through the early 1970s with Isaac Hayes, The Staple Singers, and others. *–R.U.*

Zeppelin's *Physical Graffiti* and Foghat's *Live* featured cutouts through which one could see underlying photos.

Alice Cooper, in conjunction with design house Pacific Eye & Ear, raised the ante with the *School's Out* album of 1971, creating a die-cut facsimile of a school desk and even including a pair of panties. *Billion Dollar Babies* was built to look like a snakeskin wallet complete with money clip. Fake currency, a printed lyric sleeve, and a perforated sheet of cards completed the package. Kiss, protégés of Cooper, carried on, providing more gatefolds, booklets, interlocking puzzle posters, and even a love gun in *Love Gun*.

Captain Beyond's self-titled was issued in regular sleeve but also a "lenticular" 3D edition, as was The Rolling Stones' *Their Satanic Majesties Request*. The Stones are also notorious for the real working zipper attached to the photographed pants adorning the *Sticky Fingers* sleeve. This caused problems in the racks, when the zipper would gouge the record in front of it. Also causing issue in racks was Alice Cooper's *Muscle of Love* album. Housed in a cardboard box, stores lamented that it took up too much space. Additionally, it had a faux water damage stain on it, which fooled buyers who thought their record was wrecked.

Finally, not so much a packaging characteristic but all about visual enticement nonetheless, is the use of colored vinyl, previously the domain of children's records. This gave way to the picture disc craze of the late 1970s, complaints about the sound

↓ Alice Cooper's *Billion Dollar Babies* was built to look like a snakeskin wallet complete with money clip and, natch, fake currency.

quality notwithstanding, given the challenges of creating good grooves in what was essentially clear vinyl. Popular early examples of picture discs are Boston's first album, Heart's *Magazine*, Michael Jackson's *Thriller*, and Elton John's *A Single Man*. Rush and AC/DC both offered red vinyl, Devo offered marbled, and Elvis Presley's label, RCA, offered everything always. Split Enz, with their *True Colors* album, gave us what's known as laser-etched vinyl, as did Styx with *Paradise Theatre* and Alice in Chains with *Jar of Flies*. Both laser etching and colored vinyl really took off in the modern vinyl reissue era, with many color variants (including swirl) often being offered on a single title, sometimes with specified numbered editions.

↑ Another novelty come-on, the picture disc appeared in the 1970s and has persisted to one degree or another, along with their notoriously poor sound quality.

ICONIC **COVERS**

BIRD AND DIZ • CHARLIE PARKER AND DIZZY GILLESPIE

Fully modern and presaging pop art, this characteristic David Stone Martin presentation is a tour de force of all the elements we expect from a top jazz cover in the 1950s. Evocative of the Beat Generation as well. Martin would carry on this style with celebrated sleeves for Verve as well as more for Clef. *–M.P.*

REMARKABLE **RECORD STORES**

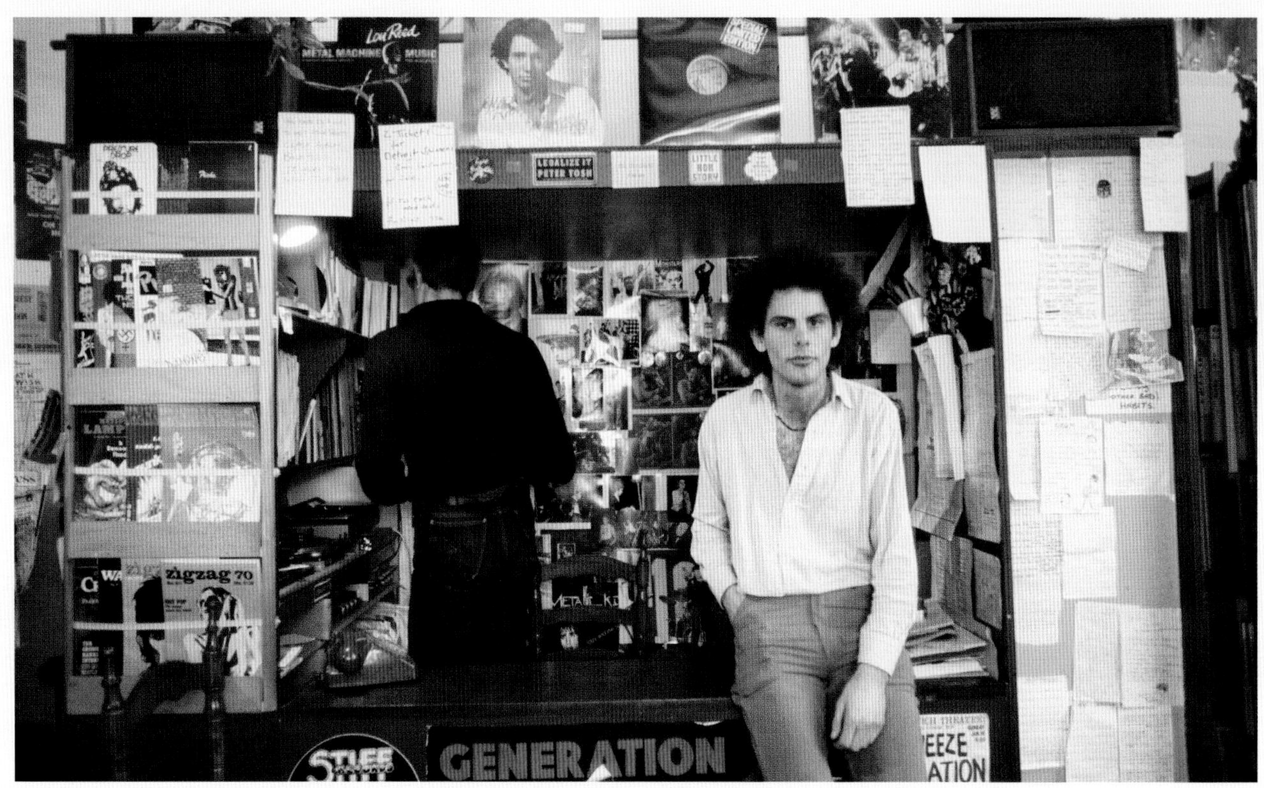

ROUGH TRADE • *LONDON, ENGLAND*

The first Rough Trade opened in Ladbrook Grove, West London, in 1976, specifically to cater to the burgeoning interest in punk, post-punk, and new wave. It was an important outlet for independent music, which larger stores at the time wouldn't carry, and quickly became a gathering place for a new generation of music fans and musicians (members of The Raincoats worked behind the counter). The shop moved to a new location in 1982, where it's now known as Rough Trade West. It also launched the label Rough Trade Records. –*G.G.*

↑ Previously the domain of children's records, colored vinyl really took off in the modern reissue era, often being offered on a single title, sometimes with specified numbered editions.

→ Two men examine the exhibition "Hyper! A Journey into Art and Music" in Hamburg, Germany. They are looking at 2,173 copies of The Beatles' "White Album" collected by artist Rutherford Chang.

Of course, all of this was designed to lure fans and more so superfans, who might buy multiple editions of the same album and maybe even frame and hang one of them on a wall. The designers at famed graphics house Hipgnosis also point out that if a fan had a multipanel Wings or Pink Floyd poster up on his or her bedroom wall, that served as a constant reminder of the album from which it originated.

THE ART OF THE LP LABEL

During the first twenty years of the vinyl LP, the label art affixed to the record itself (and punched with a spindle hole) could be pretty darn starchy—all business, humorless, functional, traditional, even kind of ugly. Hand it to those smarmy Beatles to revolutionize the use of this real estate, when *The Beatles* issued November 22, 1968, became the first full-length album on Apple Records, which conjured for a label design two distinctive sharp photographs of a sliced apple, one of the pulpy white insides and the other—cheeky of them—an outer skin that was green and not red.

Therein was established the concept of the record label as an opportunity for creativity and also representing a stamp of quality, implicit from the effort put into the design of its records. What had previously been a necessity was now a two-pronged marketing tool: The brand was strengthened, and, as a bonus, the buyer got additional art.

↑ Two vanity labels—The Beatles' Apple and Led Zeppelin's Swan Song (right page)—are notable for stepping up the design game of the labels that are physically affixed to vinyl records.

Vertigo succeeded here on both counts, as fans were mesmerized by the hypnotic swirl of its black-and-white logo as it spun 'round at 33⅓. The buyer was also predisposed to admire the music enclosed because being signed to Vertigo meant daring art rock of some sort, some kind of jazzy or heavy prog rock essentially. Then Vertigo got a makeover, with its jazzy, jagged sci-fi spaceship label being one of the most gorgeous of the 1970s. Also quite pretty were the Virgin and Charisma imprints, with Led Zeppelin's vanity label Swan Song, featuring an Icarus figure that looked like Robert Plant, nearly matching the new Vertigo art for sumptuous color and all-around pizzazz. (On the subject of "vanity" labels, neither Track, Purple, nor Rolling Stones Records looked particularly impressive by comparison.)

Also indicative of the physical label's importance was the special occasion when a storied imprint, like Dire Straits' *Brothers in Arms* and Alice Cooper's *Lace and Whiskey* for Warner Bros. or Blue Öyster Cult's *Mirrors* for Columbia, allowed their art department to mess with tradition and inject something from the band's personality into the art—or chuck the corporate brand altogether and do something completely custom. Another use of the label as an opportunity to entice the buyer is the presentation of something completely visual on side 1 (usually), with the track list and credits

for all the songs printed on the second side—Vertigo had done this with the original label as a rule, but later, this maneuver was usually album-specific.

The point, as always, was the inherent messaging, the delivery of an album with distinction and therefore more likely to attract your allowance money as you stood there in the drugstore weighing your options. Of course, you couldn't see the label under that plastic skin and cardboard sleeve; but again, perhaps even more crucial was the idea that being on Vertigo—or Verve, SST, Creation, Sub Pop, DGM, Deutsche Grammophon, or . . . —meant what was inside was going to be good.

MODERN VINYL

As alluded to in the discussion of gatefolds, there came a time when the LP was replaced by the CD. In North America, the wholesale switchover took place circa 1990, with Europe carrying on with vinyl with some level of sincerity until about 1994. Slowly but surely, however, vinyl made a comeback, albeit in low and sometimes strictly limited quantities as a sort of boutique collectible item.

Broadly speaking, there are three types of vinyl records these days. First, there are reissues of albums from the vinyl era. In most cases, record companies strive to re-create the original packaging of these titles, albeit usually with more gloss, a thicker grade of cardboard, and general attention to quality. As well, however, often there is a deluxe element involved, possibly with added inserted collectibles, due to some sort of expansion of the album that facilitates the need for a second record. Also as noted, there's much more use of color vinyl these days.

Second are standalone vinyl albums of live shows that might have previously been the domain of bootlegs, and newly generated compilations of hits or rarities. Often these are limited and maybe numbered, and sometimes they are created for the annual vinyl-promoting Record Store Day campaign.

The third category of modern-day vinyl is the issue of albums on vinyl of releases from the CD age. To put a fine distinction on it, this could mean reissues of albums from the 1990s, concurrent vinyl and CD releases from the early days of the revival (say, early 2000s; these items are often highly collectible), or, as happens today on a regular basis, an almost expected concurrent release of an album on CD and vinyl, both in greatly reduced numbers due to streaming having become the dominant method of music distribution.

What are the ramifications for packaging? Well, it's a happy story. Given that since the advent of CDs more graphics and liner notes and provided printed lyrics are expected, generally speaking, there are more gatefolds and booklets and inserts than in the old days, sometimes with the CD or a code to grab a free download thrown in as a bonus. The very presence of an offered download reveals a secret: Often these records never get played, with many collectors hesitant to even crack the cellophane. ◊

↑ A consumer browses a Brooklyn, New York, shop during Record Store Day 2014. Broadly speaking, there are three types of vinyl records these days: reissues of albums from the vinyl era; standalone vinyl albums that may include live shows and newly generated compilations; and issues of releases from the CD age.

CHAPTER 4

SHOP AROUND

DOWN AT THE RECORD STORE

BY GILLIAN G. GAAR

↑ Nothing can replace the visceral experience of going to a record store, whether to find something specific or simply to see what you might find.

You can order records through the mail. You can download music online. You can even just stream music through your phone, computer, or television set if you're interested in hearing a particular song but don't want to pay to add it to your collection. But nothing can replace the physical, visceral experience of going to a record store, whether you're there to find something specific or are simply taking your time browsing around to see what you might find.

Shops have sold recordings since the late nineteenth century, when recorded music was available only on wax cylinders. The next format, 78rpm discs, arrived by 1901; and record stores routinely made the adjustment to their stock every time a new format was developed. The 1990s might have seen vinyl disappearing from the shelves, but record stores remained. And even as music consumption steadily moved online in the twenty-first century and major record store chains around the world continued to close shop, independent stores, defying all odds, continued to hang on. The record store is still with us. And as long as people continue to buy physical media, they always will be.

IN THE BEGINNING . . .

In the beginning, there were no record stores—and not just because the first recordings to be sold were not the discs we'd later call "records." It simply wasn't financially viable to run a store that only sold musical recordings. So, the earliest recording formats—wax cylinders and then shellac 78rpm discs—were sold alongside other products, mostly in music stores that also sold phonographs, sheet music, and musical instruments.

Stores that sold appliances, including record players, were a natural outlet for selling records. But other types of businesses found that records could easily fit alongside a shop's inventory as well. The roots of the Tower Records chain date back to Russ Solomon's decision to start carrying records in his father's Sacramento drugstore, Tower Drugs. A customer who asked Sam "Goody" Gutowitz if he sold records at his New York City toy store prompted him to start carrying them; due to their strong sales, he later opened the first of what would become a chain of record stores. Department stores stocked records, often by the electronics department. In later years, large discount stores (also known as big-box retailers) like Walmart, Kmart, Costco, and Best Buy had separate music departments. Gas stations would even offer free records as an incentive to purchase gas at a particular station.

The disadvantage was that the stock at such large-scale outlets like department stores was necessarily limited due to space. Record shops in malls or chain record stores also focused on current releases, with little in the way of back catalog. This left the market wide open for stores that could cater to true music aficionados who were interested in more than simply the latest chart hits. Independently owned record stores tended to specialize in a specific musical genre (e.g., jazz, R&B, reggae, punk), and if the stores were smaller in size, they were broader in stock, carrying a deeper catalog of records, and having a more knowledgeable staff.

Used record stores offered the opportunity for even greater discoveries. Though some stores carried both new and used stock, it was more common at the time for the two entities to be separate: A shop sold either new releases or used records. Pre-internet, used record stores were the only way to locate records that were out of print, with customers going through the bins item by item. If you were

↑ Glenn Wallichs opened Wallichs Music City in Hollywood in 1940. Wallichs parlayed his success into a chain of other stores and then went on to cofound Capitol Records.

lucky, you might find what you were looking for at the first store you went to. Or you might end up going to numerous shops in search of your prize. But that was all part of the fun.

Independent stores could also play a role in shaping music history. Glenn Wallichs opened Wallichs Music City in Hollywood in 1940; singer Nat King Cole performed at the opening. It eventually became the largest record store on the West Coast, and Wallichs not only parlayed his success into a chain of other stores but went on to cofound Capitol Records along with singer and composer Johnny Mercer and Paramount production chief Buddy DeSylva. Legendary Memphis DJ Dewey Phillips helped break down racial barriers in the South by spreading the gospel of rhythm and blues and rock 'n' roll, spinning the records he'd picked up at Poplar Tunes, a.k.a. "Pop Tunes," to showcase on his nightly radio

COLUMBIA RECORDS
SIDNEY BECHETS TRIO
JIMMY RYAN'S
Really the Blues
Real Jazz
Billie Holiday
SWING

REMARKABLE **RECORD STORES**

COMMODORE RECORDS

NEW YORK, NEW YORK

The store that invented the concept of reissues. The former radio store changed its name in 1934 when it began selling jazz records full time. Store owner Milt Gabler next started the Commodore label, re-pressing out-of-print jazz recordings; it subsequently also released new recordings, including Billie Holiday's "Strange Fruit." In its heyday, the store was regarded as the top outlet for jazz recordings in the country. Commodore closed in 1959. –*G.G.*

↑ Independent stores can play a role in shaping music history. Memphis DJ Dewey Phillips helped break down racial barriers by spinning the rhythm and blues and rock 'n' roll records he picked up at Poplar Tunes.

→ Country superstar Ernest Tubb hosted the live *Midnite Jamboree* broadcast from his Nashville record store on Saturday nights.

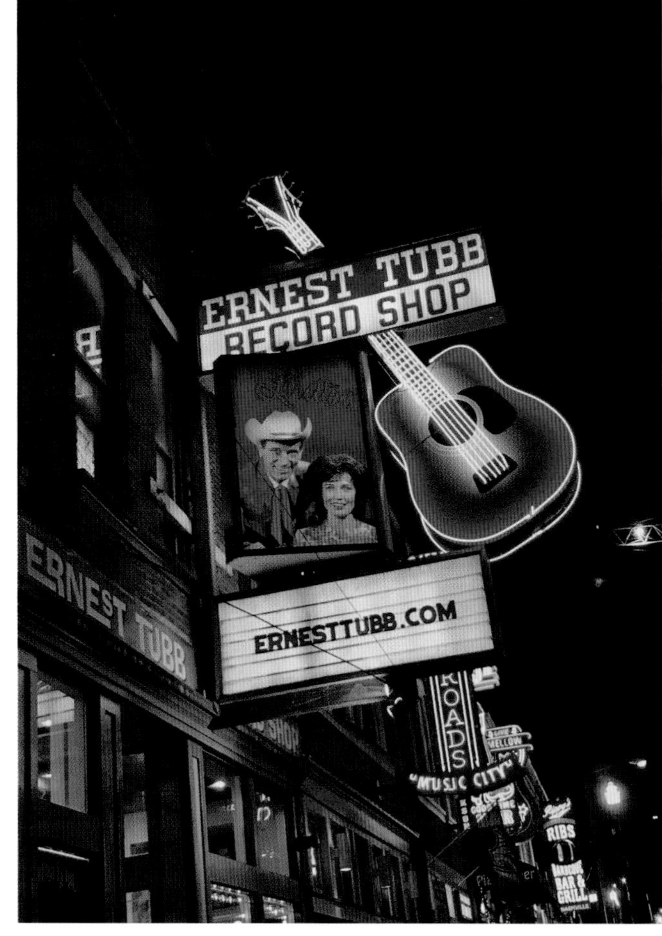

program *Red, Hot & Blue*. Country star Ernest Tubb proudly ran Ernest Tubb Record Shop in Nashville, hosting a live broadcast, *Midnite Jamboree*, that aired following the *Grand Ole Opry* broadcasts on Saturday nights. On October 2, 1954, a young man from Memphis who'd just appeared on the Opry stage made his way to the record shop to make an appearance on Tubb's show: Elvis Presley, in his first out-of-town appearance.

LEGENDARY **LABELS**

IMMEDIATE

The British recording industry was dominated by four major labels in the 1960s, Immediate marking the first notable effort to form a more artist-oriented and cutting-edge competitor, although it had major label distribution. Cofounded by Rolling Stones manager Andrew Oldham with Tony Calder, it produced hits by the Small Faces, The Nice, and Humble Pie, as well as albums with cult followings by the likes of Duncan Browne and Billy Nichols. There were also dynamic singles by John Mayall's Bluesbreakers (with Eric Clapton) and Scottish group The Poets, and a U.K. #1 hit cover of The Rolling Stones' "Out of Time" by Chris Farlowe produced by Mick Jagger. But Oldham's organizational acumen wasn't nearly as sharp as his knack for nurturing talent, and Immediate dissolved in confusing financial problems by the beginning of the 1970s. *–R.U.*

↑ "Vince Everett" signs 7-inch picture sleeves for fans in the 1957 film *Jailhouse Rock*.

← By midcentury, listening booths were a common feature of record stores, giving music fans an opportunity to listen before purchasing. Both the customer and the clerk in this 1950s Swedish store seem very intent.

→ Savvy shop owners know that customers who hang out are more likely to spend money. In Turku, Finland, 8Raita features comfortable chairs and, this being Finland, coffee and table hockey.

MORE THAN JUST SELLING RECORDS

In addition to selling music, record stores also served as something akin to a community center for music fans and musicians. Film director, screenwriter, and music journalist Cameron Crowe described a record store as "a place of escape. It was a library and a clubhouse" in the book *Record Store Days*, emphasizing that along with purchasing music, people went to record stores to make connections. Shops would have bulletin boards for musicians wanted/available ads; bands could leave flyers for upcoming gigs; fans could meet others with similar music tastes. As Penny Lane, a character in Crowe's film *Almost Famous*, says, "And if you ever get lonely, you just go to the record store and visit your friends."

Another perk record stores offered was the opportunity to listen to the records before you bought them. As early as 1924, the Wiley B. Allen store in San Francisco had record players hooked up to earphones to allow for private listening. By mid-century, listening booths were a common feature of record stores. This was something that musicians in particular took advantage of, especially young bands that might be interested in covering a specific song but didn't have sufficient funds to buy the record. Huddling in a listening booth and playing the record over and over again was a common tactic for groups like The Beatles, who would hole up in a booth armed with pencil and paper, repeatedly playing a record until they were sure they had written down all the words and chord changes correctly.

As musicians naturally spent a lot of time hanging out at record stores, it's not surprising that a number of them eventually found themselves working behind the counter as well. Before their own careers took off, you might run into James Osterberg Jr. (a.k.a. Iggy Pop) at Discount Records in Ann Arbor, Michigan; Joy Division's Ian Curtis at Rare Records, in Manchester, England; Wilco's Jeff Tweedy at Euclid Records in suburban St. Louis;

ICONIC **COVERS**

RIO • DURAN DURAN

It's only the spring of 1982, but here it is, an album cover to represent the dominant look of the 1980s. It features a painting by American artist Patrick Nagel, who was influenced by art deco, pop art, and Japanese woodblock printing. Nagel would suffer from a heart attack less than two years later, dying at the age of 38. *–M.P.*

→ Metallica rocks the racks at Rasputin Music in Berkeley, California, on Record Store Day 2016. "In-stores" are usually tied to a new release or an upcoming show. Best of all, they are almost always free.

or Hüsker Dü's Grant Hart and Greg Norton at Northern Lights in St. Paul, Minnesota. Patti Smith met her future guitarist, Lenny Kaye, when he was working as a clerk at Village Oldies in New York City. Guitarist Peter Buck was working at Wuxtry Records in Athens, Georgia, when he made friends with a customer named Michael Stipe, with whom he'd go on to cofound R.E.M.

Record stores also served as performing venues. Some stores, like Ernest Tubb Record Shop and Dolphin's of Hollywood, held live radio broadcasts right in the store. Musicians also made personal appearances, eventually known as "in-stores," to sign autographs, play a short set, or both. In-stores were usually tied to a promotional event like a new record release or an upcoming show. Best of all, they were almost always free.

Many up-and-coming acts do in-stores as a means of generating attention. The Go-Go's first in-stores accompanied the release of their major label debut, *Beauty and the Beat*; and during Nirvana's 1991 tour promoting *Nevermind*, the band made a number of in-store appearances along the way (the band had long been a fan of in-stores, making their first such appearance at Rhino Records in Los Angeles on June 23, 1989). Some performers—Paul McCartney, Patti Smith, Elvis Costello, and Foo Fighters among them—have continued to make in-store appearances long after they've found success, simply because they enjoy the excitement of performing in an intimate venue to their most loyal fans.

THE RISE OF THE CHAIN STORE

As 78s gave way to 7-inch 45s and 12-inch LPs, record sales boomed—and record stores expanded accordingly. HMV's flagship store in London boasted it was the largest record store in the world, and soon chain stores arose to challenge that dominance. The first chain record store in the United States was the National Record Mart (NRM), founded in Pittsburgh, Pennsylvania. Hyman Shapiro, along with his sons Sam and Howard, had opened their first store, Jitterbug Records, in 1937. By 1941 they owned three stores, changed the name to the National Record Mart, and expanded beyond the state line in the 1970s.

Tower Records became arguably the best-known chain record store in the United States. After getting his start selling records at Tower Drugs, Russ Solomon opened the first Tower Records store in Sacramento in 1960. Seven years later, he opened his first out-of-town store in San Francisco; and expansion continued from there, eventually moving into overseas markets.

Tower Records changed the idea of what a chain store could be. There was no corporate-mandated

↑ [top] As vinyl increased in popularity, record stores grew accordingly. Sam Goody (pictured) became one of the better-known chains in the United States.

↑ [bottom] Dolly Parton greets fans at Peaches Records & Tapes in Atlanta, Georgia, in 1977. Peaches expanded to forty-five shops in major U.S. markets.

LEGENDARY **LABELS**

ISLAND

Island began primarily as an outlet for Jamaican ska and early reggae in the United Kingdom in the early to mid-1960s. But after Chris Blackwell, the label's principal guiding force, had some success in the rock market with mid-1960s hits by The Spencer Davis Group, Island moved into British psychedelic and progressive rock with Traffic; King Crimson; Emerson, Lake & Palmer; and Roxy Music, as well as folk-rock with Cat Stevens, Fairport Convention, and Nick Drake. Always mindful of his Jamaican reggae roots, Blackwell was crucial to crossing Bob Marley and the Wailers over to the pop/rock market in the mid-1970s and continued to have big Island hits with artists ranging from U2 to Grace Jones, also helping introduce African music to American/European audiences with the likes of King Sunny Ade. He tells his side of the story in his memoir, *The Islander*. *–R.U.*

ICONIC **COVERS**

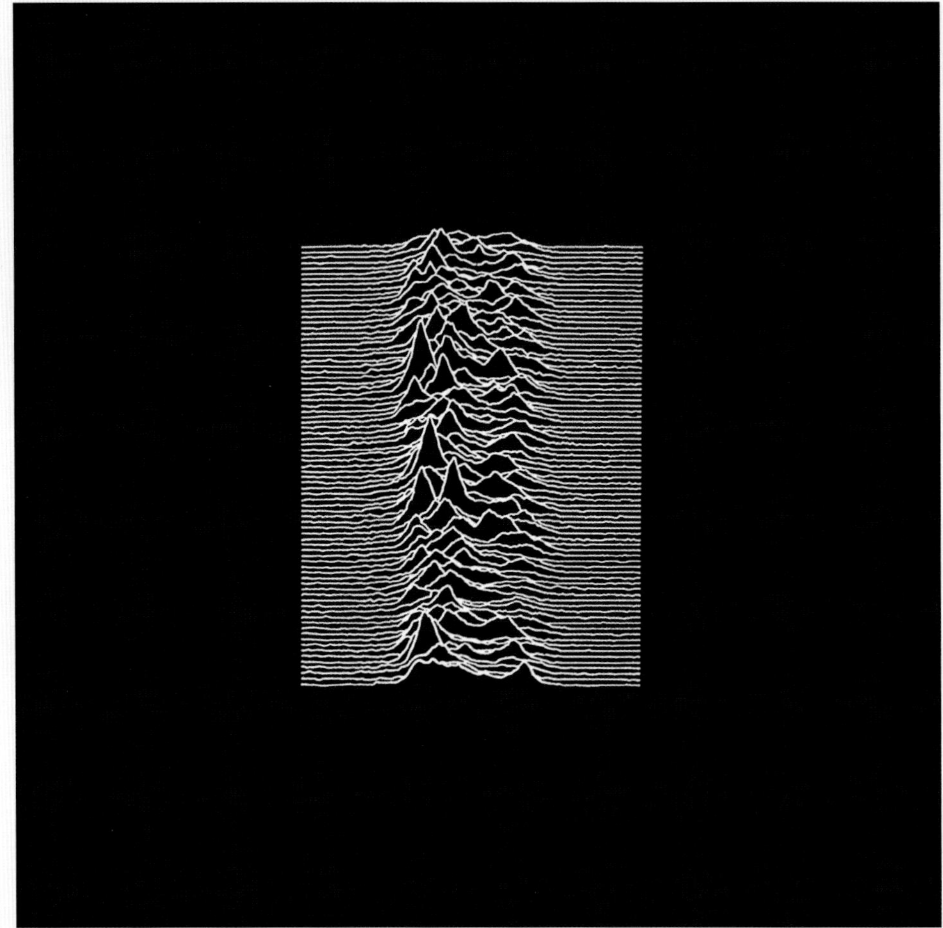

UNKNOWN PLEASURES • JOY DIVISION

We can thank Factory Records designer Peter Saville for the image used on Joy Division's somber debut album, depicting radio waves from a pulsar star and created by astronomer Harold Craft. The band liked it better in its original black-on-white composition, but Saville thought it looked "sexier" this way. It's indeed lived on to be seen on T-shirts the world over, with no supporting text, which is another daring element of this simple sleeve. *–M.P.*

→ Chain stores flourished in the United States from the 1970s to the 1990s, emboldening large U.K. chains like HMV (His Master's Voice) to move into major U.S. cities.

one-size-fits-all approach to doing business. Stores were encouraged to cater to local tastes and interests. Employees were knowledgeable about music and happy to pass on suggestions and recommendations. There was also just the sheer size of Tower stores, the sight of thousands of records on display making record buyers' eyes gleam in anticipation. The stores filled their windows with huge reproductions of album covers, adding to the visual excitement. It was a large-scale store that nonetheless fostered an independent spirit and attitude.

Following Tower's example, chain stores flourished in the United States from the 1970s to the 1990s. The large U.K. chains HMV (His Master's Voice) and Virgin Megastores moved in, opening outlets in major U.S. cities. The first Peaches Records & Tapes opened in Atlanta, Georgia, in 1975, eventually expanding to forty-five shops in major U.S. markets. Some of their stores rivaled Tower and Virgin Megastores in terms of size, and they added a touch of showbiz flair by having performers like The Beach Boys, Dolly Parton, The Allman Brothers, and Willie Nelson leave their handprints in cement outside select stores. The store also sold specially designed wooden crates with a label featuring the store's logo (two Georgia peaches) to hold records (though most Peaches stores have closed, you can still order the crates from peachesrecordcrates.com). Other chains included Sam Goody, Wherehouse Music, FYE (For Your Entertainment), Camelot Music and The Wall (the two brand names of the same company, whose stores were primarily in malls in the Southeast and Midwest), and Coconuts (a Midwest chain). Though popular, these chains tended to lack the distinctive character of a Tower or Peaches; they were stores for more casual consumers instead of hardcore music fans.

A HIT!
'YOU MIGHT AS WELL FORGET HIM'
'ITS AS SIMPLE AS THAT'
Tommy Quickly
7N 35183
CILLA'S GREATEST!
'YOU'RE MY WORLD'
'SUFFER NOW I MUST'
Available NOW
NEMS TOP TWENTY
DIONNE WARWICK
BOB DYLAN

REMARKABLE **RECORD STORES**

NEMS (NORTH END MUSIC STORE)

LIVERPOOL, ENGLAND

Even without its links to The Beatles, the Whitechapel branch of the Epstein family's chain of stores merits attention for its status as "the finest record selection in the North" (of England). The main floor's ceiling was decorated with album covers, the first shop in the nation to have this soon-much-copied feature. The store's policy was to order any record a customer requested, which is what led the shop's manager, Brian Epstein, to order a single that The Beatles appeared on as backing musicians. He ended up becoming the group's manager. The chain closed in the 1970s. –*G.G.*

ICONIC **COVERS**

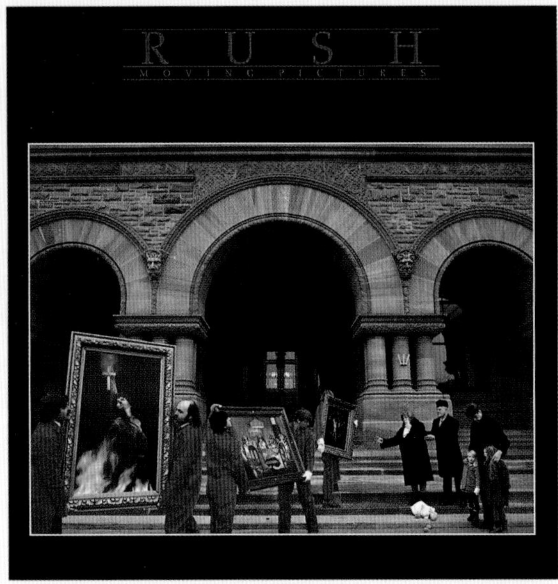

MOVING PICTURES

RUSH

Many of Hugh Syme's packaging designs for Rush and others are celebrated for sly visual puns. But *Moving Pictures* takes the cake: The scene depicts a moving picture company filming movers moving pictures while onlookers are moved by the moving pictures. As a bonus, the cover helped turn Ontario's provincial headquarters into a top Toronto tourist attraction. *–M.P.*

ADAPTING TO CDS

On October 1, 1982, Billy Joel's *52nd Street* became the first compact disc ever sold when it was released in Japan. The silver discs quickly caught on, and by 1988, they surpassed the sales of vinyl records. Record stores had no problem adapting, replacing bins that once held vinyl albums and 7-inch singles with CD-sized racks. Then record distributors changed their return policies for vinyl, charging more for returns and providing more incentive to carry CDs. By the 1990s, it became common for albums to be released only on CD and cassette.

Another change in the music industry was the adoption of SoundScan in determining chart placings. Previously industry publications like *Billboard* worked out chart placings based on sales information provided by specific stores. As there was little oversight of the process, the sales reports could easily be manipulated, with those who compiled the reports offered "gifts" in return for reporting higher sales for a record. SoundScan was based on actual sales, from scanning a release's barcode.

Now sales became even more of a numbers game for major labels, and chain stores followed their lead—even outlets like Tower shifted their focus to Top 40 releases. Big-box retailers had always focused on major releases, but now the chains were starting to lose more of their individuality.

Sales of CDs peaked in 2000, when compact discs comprised 92 percent of all music format sales. But a new day was dawning with the rise of MP3s and file sharing. It was the first time a new music format was not a physical object that you could hold in your hand. Suddenly it wasn't just a matter of installing a different sized bin for a new format. This was a product that didn't need to be

↑ By 1988 compact discs surpassed vinyl records in sales. Record stores had no problem replacing bins that once held vinyl albums and 7-inch singles with CD-sized racks.

sold in a physical store at all. CDs had squeezed vinyl records out of stores. Now MP3s were squeezing out the stores themselves.

But there was more at play than simply the arrival of the digital revolution. In a way, CDs became a victim of their own success. Big-box retailers like Walmart and Target began using them as loss leaders, selling them for substantially less than a chain like Tower or Wherehouse. Such stores could afford to lose money by selling CDs cheaply, as their primary profits came from the other goods they sold. This led to the perception that CDs were the kind of impulse purchase that you threw into your cart at the last minute, like a candy bar. But record stores couldn't afford to cut their prices to match those of non–record store retailers. It put them in a financial bind.

Chains also fell prey to their own poor decisions. Tower Records, for example, expanded too quickly at a time of falling profits and ended up declaring bankruptcy. Other chains followed, with Virgin Megastores and HMV eventually closing all their stores in the United States. Consolidation also put an end to a number of chains. Transworld Entertainment swallowed up FYE, Wherehouse, Camelot Music, Coconuts, and Sam Goody and ended up closing most of the shops. Independents were better placed to survive; specialist stores tended to attract a loyal clientele and had deeper back catalogs. But online sales of records also took a toll, as increasing numbers of people who still wanted to buy physical product could now do so without even leaving their homes.

As sales of physical media dropped, record stores continued to close. But the fact that people were buying records online meant there was still a market, however reduced, for physical product. How could these people be lured back into the stores? Some people who thought they might have an idea put their heads together.

→ London shoppers browse the Record Store Day releases in 2019.

RECORD STORE DAY

On September 22, 2007, Chris Brown (of Bull Moose Music in Portland, Maine) and Eric Levin (of the vinyl-only Criminal Records in Atlanta) gathered together with a select group of record store owners (Michael Kurtz, Carrie Colliton, Brian Poehner, Don Van Cleave, and Amy Dorfman) at the Sound Garden record store in the Baltimore neighborhood of Fell's Point to think up new ways they might reach out to record buyers. They came up with the idea of hosting an event: Record Store Day.

It was a simple concept: Make special releases that were only available for purchase in stores. "This is a day for the people who make up the world of the record store—the staff, the customers, and the artists—to come together and celebrate the unique culture of a record store and the special role [these independently owned stores] play in their communities," the event's website stated. And what better way to make record buyers "come together" than to offer exclusive limited-edition releases? (A similar approach had been used in establishing Free Comic Book Day.) Part of the fun of perusing the offerings at a record store had always been the chance to stumble across a special rarity. Record Store Day would be like a vinyl Easter egg hunt, drawing customers in the hopes of snagging a record that you wouldn't be able to get anywhere else.

The first Record Store Day (RSD) was held on Saturday, April 19, 2008. Around 300 U.S. record stores participated, and the event went international as well: Cofounder Michael Kurtz flew to the United Kingdom to kick off the event with Billy Bragg. Metallica was the first big act to make an in-store appearance at RSD, drawing hundreds to

↑ Phil Wilcox, manager at Tres Gatos Bookstore in Boston, sorted through limited-edition releases in preparation for Record Store Day 2018. RSD is like a vinyl Easter egg hunt, drawing customers in the hopes of snagging records that they can't get anywhere else.

→ A vinyl lover pauses with their RSD haul at Rough Trade East in London, 2019.

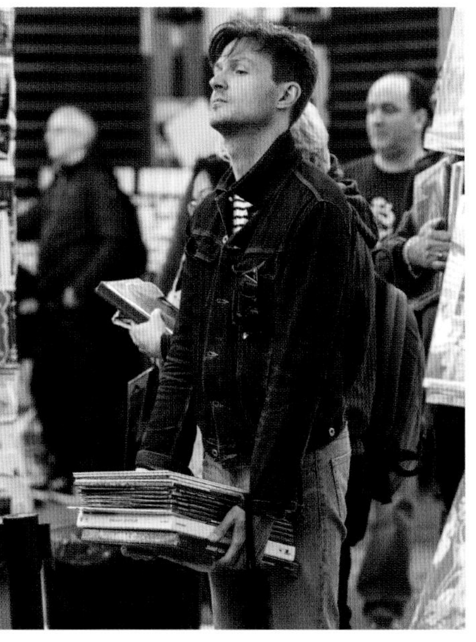

Rasputin Music (fittingly, a former Tower Records location) in Mountain View, California. Among the special releases that first year were records by R.E.M., Stephen Malkmus, Death Cab for Cutie, Vampire Weekend, Black Kids, Jason Mraz, and The Teenagers. There would come to be three types of RSD releases: exclusives, which were only available at independent record stores; "RSD Firsts," which were initially sold at RSD stores prior to being sold at other outlets; and small run/regional titles, which were only sold in specific regions or were in small runs of under a thousand. Releases could be reissues of records long out of print, previously unreleased material, or a new record that would later go into general release. Colored vinyl and picture discs were added enticements.

RSD organizers encouraged participating stores to make the event about more than simply selling records. Live DJs, in-store appearances, musicians

→ RSD has received some criticism over the years, especially as more major labels signed on for the event and independent labels began to feel crowded out.

taking shifts working behind the counter, raffles, contests, and giveaways turned the day into a party. The event eventually spread to every continent in the world except Antarctica.

Beginning in 2009, a yearly ambassador was chosen to be the public face of the event. Jesse Hughes, lead singer for Eagles of Death Metal, was the ambassador in 2009. Subsequent ambassadors have included Ozzy Osbourne, Chuck D, Pearl Jam, and Brandi Carlisle. A secondary event, RSD Black Friday (the first Friday after Thanksgiving), was launched in 2010. And in 2016, the first RSD Summer Camp was held—a conference for record store owners, staff, distributors, vendors, and "anyone whose work places them in the orbit of a record store," now an annual event that's "devoted to the unique business that is the independent record store." The COVID-19 pandemic canceled the April 2020 event, but RSD quickly rebounded, with "RSD Drops" rescheduled for August 29, September 26, and October 24 that year, as well as the usual RSD Black Friday on November 27. Multiple drops continued in 2021 and 2022.

RSD has generated some controversy. Some have disliked the event's prioritizing collectors over the casual record buyer. As more major labels signed on for the event, independent labels began to feel crowded out. And, of course, there were the profiteers who scooped up the most desirable releases, then listed them on online sites like eBay at two to three times their original price.

In an article in *The Guardian*, a record store owner identified as Rupert contended that the production of releases for RSD had led to delays in the production of non-RSD records, exacerbated by vinyl shortages and shipping delays. "The administrative ramifications are hugely consuming for shops, and the economic impact for independent artists and labels is devastating," he wrote. "In-store tours—crucial for promotion and first-week sales—have been canceled and rescheduled; artists are missing out on the chart positions they should expect; entire summer touring schedules are being scrapped because there is such uncertainty about when the physical product will materialize."

ICONIC **COVERS**

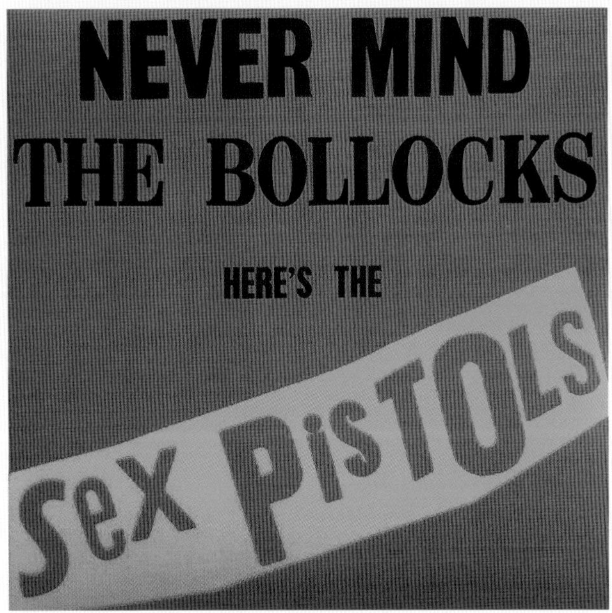

NEVER MIND THE BOLLOCKS, HERE'S THE SEX PISTOLS

THE SEX PISTOLS

The definitive punk album came housed in punk's definitive cover, making use of crude cut-and-paste and sort of "serial killer" lettering for the band name. It also has a lurid palette and is festooned with a naughty word, "bollocks," English slang for testicles. –M.P.

But the organization has also been honored for its accomplishments. Michael Kurtz was made a "Knight" of the Ordre des Arts et des Lettres (Order of the Arts and Letters) by France in 2013. "In a statement on receiving the award, Kurtz said record store owners are like recording artists because they choose longevity over a quick profit and embrace the soulful experience of building a great store because they want their customers to feel the joy and energy from music, just like music artists do when they create their music," *Billboard* reported. The same year, NARM (National Recording Association of Merchandisers, now the Music Business Association) gave the organization the Independent Spirit Award; RSD was also named Marketplace Ally of the Year by A2IM (American Association of Independent Music) in 2015.

Most importantly, RSD is credited with helping to kick-start a resurgence of interest in vinyl—and the importance of buying that vinyl in stores. "Record Store Day's efforts on behalf of independent record stores, particularly its annual Record Store Day event, personify the independent spirit and have been enthusiastically embraced by artists and fans alike, leading to increased awareness and sales for these important but often overlooked physical institutions," Jim Donio, then president of NARM, told *Billboard* in 2013.

THE FUTURE

While sales of digital music steadily increased and CD sales continued to decline, sales of vinyl have continued to rebound, leading Sony Music in 2018 to begin manufacturing vinyl records in-house again for the first time since 1989. By 2020 (pre-pandemic), vinyl began outselling CDs for the first time since the 1980s. In 2021, one out of every three albums sold in the United States was on vinyl.

This brought vinyl back to the shelves—where shelves were available. While physical media has managed to hang on in the face of the digital onslaught, the number of record stores in the United States continues to decline. According to IBISWorld, there were 1,912 record stores in the United States in 2022, a 6.8 percent decline from 2021. Some of those closures were undoubtedly due to the pandemic, which impacted independently owned businesses in particular.

↑ Kimberly Baugh waits on customers at Jack White's Third Man Records on Record Store Day 2015 in Nashville, Tennessee. Vinyl hounds were able to buy a 10-inch, 78rpm facsimile of Elvis Presley's original recording of "My Happiness" and "That's When Your Heartaches Begin"—with all the pops and crackles of the original acetate.

DOLPHIN'S HIT PARADE
FRAGILE
FRAGILE

REMARKABLE **RECORD STORES**

DOLPHIN'S OF HOLLYWOOD

LOS ANGELES, CALIFORNIA

Located in South Central Los Angeles, the name of John Dolphin's store was a subtle jab at the segregationist polices of the time (1951) that wouldn't allow him to open a store in Hollywood. It became an immediate center for the city's jazz and R&B scene, where you might run into the likes of Billie Holiday, Sam Cooke, and James Brown. There were live radio broadcasts from the store, which was open twenty-four hours a day. The store closed in 1989. Dolphin's life inspired the musical *Recorded in Hollywood*. –G.G.

↑ In contrast to the United States, the number of record shops in the United Kingdom has increased in recent years. Unfortunately Long Play Café in Grainger Market, Newcastle upon Tyne, was not one of those that survived the pandemic.

But there are bright spots. In contrast to the United States, the number of record shops in the United Kingdom has increased in recent years. And, as always, record stores are adapting, just as they did when LPs and 45s replaced 78s and CDs replaced (for a moment, anyway) vinyl. Chain stores are mostly gone, though Tower Records returned as an online-only retailer. And there are fewer retailers carrying music at all (with some exceptions, like Urban Outfitters, which carries vinyl releases). So, it's been left to independents to figure out how to help the modern-day record store survive.

The answer is looking for new ways to stay relevant. Today's independent stores are more likely to carry both new and used releases, a variety of formats (you can still find 8-track tapes lurking in the dark back corners of some shops), related ephemera like T-shirts, merchandise with the shop's logo, and books and magazines, as well as having an affiliated website for online sales. The store might also share space with a restaurant or a bar (such as The Record Café in Bradford, England, whose website boasts that it offers "Vinyl, Ale, Ham"). There are stores that sell memberships, pop-ups that are open only on the weekends, even a moving record shop on a barge (The Record Deck) that travels up and down the rivers and canals of southern England. And there's still a Peaches Records open in New Orleans.

When e-books came along, it was said they would be the end of the physical book. But after an initial burst, sales of e-books plateaued and never surpassed those of physical books. It's the same with record stores. Downloading, streaming, and ordering music online are all wonderful conveniences. But they can't replace the tantalizing *human* experience of walking into a record store, nodding hello to your friends and fellow music fans, getting a few recommendations from the clerk, picking up a flyer for an upcoming show, tapping your foot to whatever music is playing on the in-house stereo, and wandering down the aisles to look through the bins, excited about the opportunity of discovering another new treasure. ◊

CHAPTER 5

BRINGING IT ALL BACK HOME

RECORD-COLLECTING CULTURE

BY MATT ANNISS

↑ So you've become a vinyl junkie. Congratulations . . . you've helped usher the format back to heights last seen in the early 1980s.

There was once a time, not that long ago, when being a dedicated record collector was a deeply unfashionable pursuit. Following the rise of the CD and, later, digital downloads, vinyl collectors were often portrayed as obsessive, antisocial oddballs whose relationship with an outdated format bordered on the unusual. Record collectors, critics argued, prioritized the medium itself over the music cut into its grooves, with urban myths about people leaving vinyl albums unplayed to protect their future commercial value cited as evidence.

How times have changed. Today vinyl sales are booming, with the Recording Industry Association of America (RIAA), according to *Variety*, reporting that sales of new records garnered over $1 billion in revenue in 2021—the first time that has been achieved since the format's "glory days" in the 1980s. Record collecting flourished during the global COVID-19 pandemic, as music fans suffering through lockdowns spent spare cash on new and old records, hi-fi equipment, and vinyl accessories.

Academic research suggests that not only did music listening soar through the pandemic, but many people either returned to physical formats—vinyl or CD—or embraced them for the first time. While it's no surprise to find dedicated collectors dealing with the pressures of the pandemic by retreating into their record rooms, many would not have expected COVID-19 to deliver a whole new generation of vinyl addicts.

"I was absolutely itching to build a collection," Portland-based student and vinyl convert Will Emanuel told *The Economic Times* in a 2021 report on the rise in record collecting during the pandemic. "I fell in a rabbit hole, and it seems I can't escape."

Those of us infected with the record collecting bug will empathize with this young collector's comments. After all, acquiring, keeping, and managing a collection of vinyl albums has long been our addiction. Naturally the music industry is keen to keep us addicted and has responded to growing demand.

Record labels regularly license and reissue rare, in-demand items, while highly limited pressings of a few hundred or a couple of thousand units appear in online stores and disappear within minutes. In March 2021, according to *Jezebel*, film soundtrack specialists Mondo announced the release of 5,000 copies of Daft Punk's soundtrack to sci-fi movie *Tron: Legacy*; they sold out within minutes of the label listing them on its website.

While lots of those who grabbed copies of that release weren't dedicated collectors but rather "flippers"—entrepreneurs who buy up new releases and then sell them for inflated prices using online marketplaces—there's no denying that record labels rely on the growing global community of record collectors to shift units. Because of this, products aimed at collectors, such

↑ Music listening soared during the pandemic, with many people turning to physical formats for the first time.

→ Acquiring and managing a collection are part of the vinyl addiction.

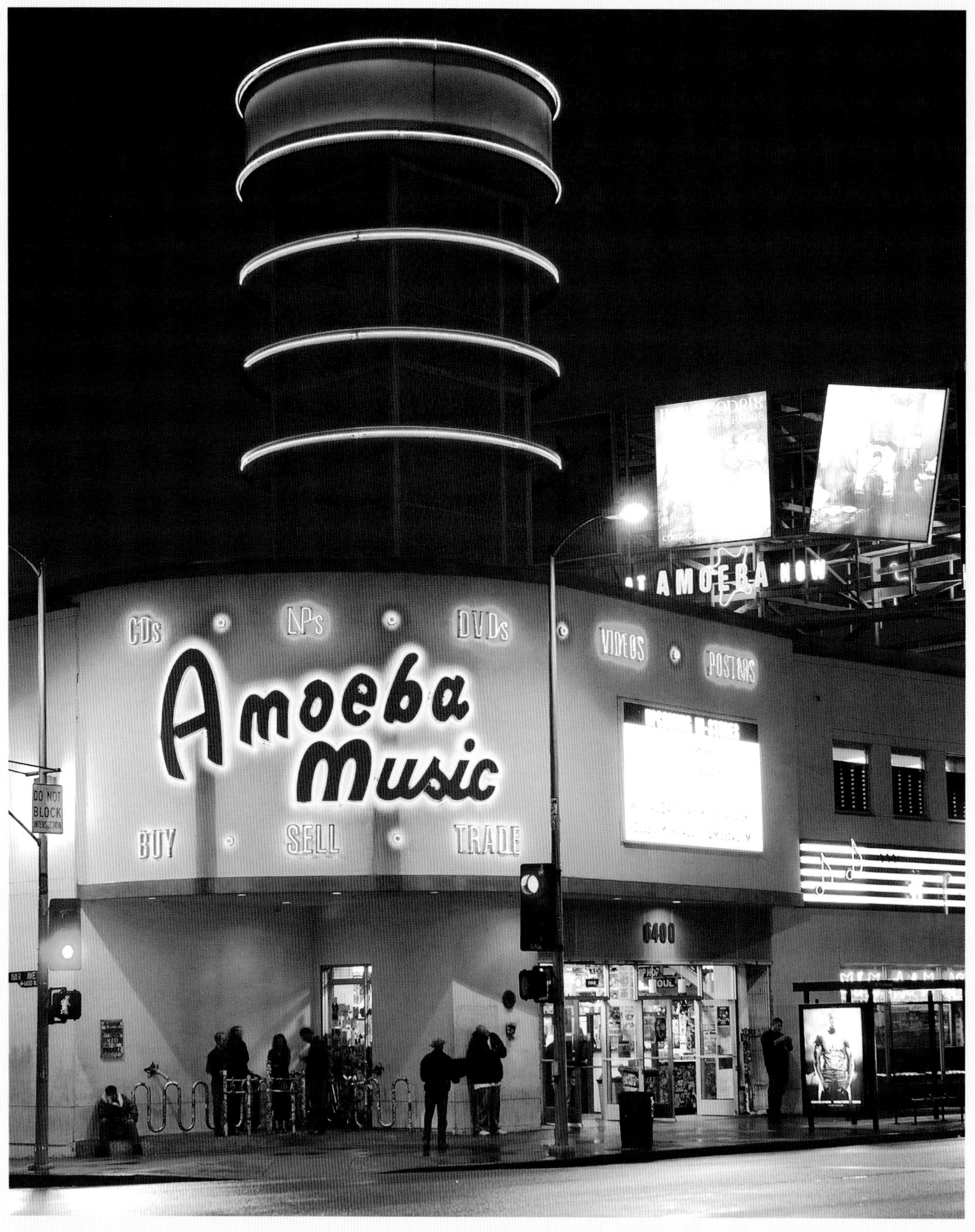
CDs
LPs
DVDs
VIDEOS
POSTERS
Amoeba
Music
BUY
SELL
TRADE
AMOEBA NOW
DO NOT BLOCK
6400

REMARKABLE **RECORD STORES**

AMOEBA MUSIC

LOS ANGELES, CALIFORNIA

The first Amoeba Music store opened in Oakland in 1990; the Los Angeles branch opened on Sunset Boulevard in 2001. The store focuses on vintage recordings, making it a huge draw for collectors. In-stores are popular—Paul McCartney's 2007 appearance was later released on the album *Amoeba Gig*. When the store was forced to close during the COVID-19 pandemic, a fund-raiser helped pay the bills until the store reopened on Hollywood Boulevard in 2021. –G.G.

as deluxe, beautifully packaged box sets of classic albums, colored vinyl pressings, and picture discs, are appearing much more regularly in stores.

For proof, just check the number of "super-deluxe" vinyl box sets of Beatles albums. Over the last decade, Apple Records has dropped expensive, lusciously packaged versions of *Sgt. Pepper's Lonely Hearts Club Band*, *The Beatles* (better known as the "White Album"), *Abbey Road*, *Let It Be*, and *Revolver*. Beatles records are not hard to find—millions were sold in the 1960s, and vinyl reissues have frequently appeared on and off ever since—yet the clamor from collectors to snap up these expanded, special-edition boxes has been predictably high. After all, for some collectors, rarity and prestige are important, though this is far from the only reason why people become immersed in vinyl culture.

ICONIC **COVERS**

MY WAR

BLACK FLAG

Raymond Pettibon did many covers for the SST label, but this is the first full-length (depending whether you call the Minutemen's *What Makes a Man Start Fires?* a full-length or not. Later, however, we'd see the signature devastating line or two of text to go along with his society-gone-berserk images. Pettibon also worked with Sonic Youth, and, much later, Foo Fighters. –*M.P.*

THE PSYCHOLOGY OF RECORD COLLECTING

So, why do people collect records? Over the years, lots of psychologists and sociologists have written academic articles and research papers about record collecting. Few agree with the traditional view of record collectors being compulsive, antisocial eccentrics. In fact, most agree that most collectors are inspired by a deep love of music and a desire to maintain a kind of physical history of their relationship with it. This is as true for young record collectors—people of a generation that initially grew up with instant access to music via streaming and digital downloads—as it is for those who first started buying LPs in the 1960s, 1970s, or 1980s.

"I'll keep buying more records that I like, and even if I don't like the band later, I'll keep the vinyl anyway because at some point I did like them," a twenty-one-year-old collector called Eddie explained in a 2017 research paper by Jack Ellis. "It's like a chronological order of stuff that I listen to. I'll always go back to it as a personal history. I've always loved music, so having that there gives me a perspective of what I've been into."

Ask fifty record collectors why they dedicate such time to their hobby and why they love vinyl and you'll get a wide variety of answers. Some cite the way the music sounds in comparison to digital music, the smell of a freshly pressed record being slid out of an inner sleeve, the feel of holding an album in your hands, or the allure of a release's packaging and artwork.

For others, it's about "completism" (the desire to own everything released by an artist or on a particular record label), the thrill of hunting down obscurities, or merely surrounding themselves

↑ Flea markets and record shows are evidence that not all collectors fall under the stereotype of cranky recluse.

LEGENDARY **LABELS**

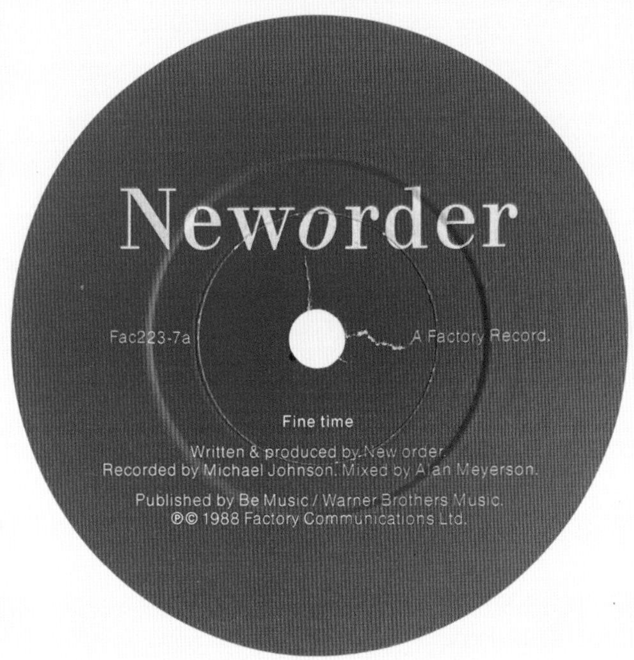

FACTORY

One of numerous labels with a sharp, often stark visual and musical identity to emerge from the punk/new wave explosion, Factory was crucial to popularizing the alternative rock sprouting from its Manchester base. It might be best known as the home of Joy Division and their spinoff group New Order but also put out seminal post-punk records by Durutti Column and A Certain Ratio. Factory cofounder Tony Wilson was a well-known television host before (and even after) the label started and also founded and managed Manchester's Haçienda club, bringing a multimedia dimension to his championship of the local music scene that even generated a popular biopic of sorts, *24 Hour Party People*. Factory had big British success in the late 1980s with Happy Mondays yet declared bankruptcy in 1992. *–R.U.*

↑ Swapping mixtapes has proven a tried-and-true method for vinyl collectors to share music with friends.

with objects that reflect a lifelong love affair with progressive rock, jazz, dance music, or incredible orchestral performances.

For some, it's a way of becoming part of a community of collectors and like-minded music fans across the globe—people whose passion for acquiring, looking after, and listening to "wax" burns as brightly as your own. As academic and lifelong record collector Kevin M. Moist wrote in his book *Contemporary Collecting: Objects, Practices, and the Fate of Things*, being a vinyl obsessive is actually far more sociable than other hobbies that involve collecting items: "Collectors, in my experience, generally love to share what they find, with friends via listening sessions or by swapping mixes, or more publicly as DJs or music writers. They would agree with rock musician Jeff Connolly that the whole point is 'using the music': 'There is no joy in ownership,' he said. 'The joy comes when you play the record.'"

Fundamentally, record collecting is a joyous hobby, whether you're an obsessive with a room, house, or storage locker full of vintage LPs or merely someone with fifty or sixty choice albums

↑ Joe Bussard of Frederick, Maryland, was a longtime collector of 78rpm records. He amassed one of the largest and most important private collections in the U.S.

neatly filed away in the shelves in your living room. While there are plenty of die-hard collectors who spend a lifetime building enormous collections, many others prefer to keep a small but manageable selection of records in pristine condition. Some collectors merely follow their favorite bands and singers or acquire albums in their preferred styles of music, while others are dedicated only to certain types of records. For example, Italian vinyl obsessive Alessandro Benedetti secured a Guinness World Record in 2010 by proving that he owned more than 1,500 colored vinyl records, 1,300 of which were LPs.

Another famous collector, the late Joe Bussard, became celebrated worldwide after building up an astonishingly large archive of 10-inch 78rpm records—the preferred vinyl format before the invention of the 12-inch LP that plays at 33⅓ rpm. He bought and sold records for a living and claimed that over 50,000 different 78s had passed through his collection. According to the *New York Times*, before he died in October 2022, he said that he'd kept

15,000 of these, most of which, dustandgrooves.com reported, were historic jazz, blues, country, and bluegrass recordings.

During his lifetime, Bussard was happy to let other collectors and music fans come to his house to listen to items from his collection. He also showcased some of them via his regular radio show, which emphasizes the point that many keen collectors are music evangelists at heart.

Bussard had plenty of rivals in the "obsessive vinyl hoarder" stakes. Bob George and his friend David Wheeler, both obsessive collectors, joined forces in 1985 to create the New York–based ARChive of Contemporary Music. "I had 47,000 recordings, which I thought had some value," George told the *New York Times* in 2009. "Somebody had to save this. But people had a hard time accepting commercially released sound recordings as valid cultural artifacts."

REMARKABLE **RECORD STORES**

TOWER RECORDS • TOKYO, JAPAN

Tower stores are still open in Japan, as the subsidiary Tower Records Japan (TRJ) became independent from the main company in 2002, thus avoiding the bankruptcy of the U.S.-based chain. The shop in Tokyo's Shibuya City neighborhood is said to be the largest record store in the world. Over the nine floors, you'll find more CDs than vinyl, a café, a performing stage, and an art gallery. –G.G.

↑ Supercollector Paul Mawhinney showed off a rare Rolling Stones album at his record shop, Record-Rama, in Pittsburgh, Pennsylvania, in 1983.

George's idea was to find, acquire, and store two copies of every record ever made—an admirable if likely impossible task, given the volume of vinyl albums and singles released over the course of the last century. Nearly four decades have passed since the ARChive was established, and it now contains more than 3 million items—around the same number as celebrated record collector Paul Mawhinney hoarded over a forty-year period.

Mawhinney, who was particularly interested in oddities and obscurities, eventually sold his entire collection to an anonymous buyer—a man who had, according to a 2014 *New York Times* report, spent the previous few years buying "deadstock" from shuttered secondhand record stores and the cherished collections of renowned collectors across the United States.

The man in question was Zero Freitas, a wealthy Brazilian who had decided to take his lifelong record collecting habit to dizzying new heights. It was his ambition to create a collection, housed in several vast warehouses in São Paulo, that contained at least one copy of every record released to date.

↑ Mawhinney eventually sold his collection of 3 million items to Zero Freitas, a wealthy Brazilian whose stated aim is to own one copy of every record released to date.

As of 2016, Freitas's collection contained more than 6 million different records, which he intends to turn into a listenable online archive. Remarkably Freitas doesn't think he's the owner of the world's largest collection either; in 2016, he told The Vinyl Factory website that he believed there were wealthy private collectors in India who may have millions more records than he does!

ON A VINYL HUNT

What Freitas, Mawhinney, and other excessive collectors have in common—aside from the financial means to allow them to go to extreme lengths to feed their vinyl habit—is an unflinching drive to find and acquire records. These kinds of collectors, and many who have the same dedication but not the money or storage space to keep more than a few thousand records at any one time, are partly driven by the thrill of the chase.

These collectors think nothing of traveling to far-flung corners of the world to hunt for records. Plenty of DJs do this too. Gilles Peterson, who has been a fixture on BBC Radio since the 1990s, regularly travels to South America and the Caribbean to find records to add to his 30,000-strong collection (jazz and Latin music are two of his specialties), *The Guardian* reported, while the entire culture of the "northern soul" club scene in the United Kingdom was built on DJs finding and sharing rare Black American soul records.

While some of these DJs bought records from dealers—people who buy and sell rare records for a living—most of the scene's leading lights (Wigan Casino resident DJ Richard Searling included) made regular record-hunting trips to the United States during the scene's commercial height in the 1970s. Ian Levine, one of the most celebrated DJs on the northern soul scene, reportedly brought thousands of rare soul records back to the United Kingdom following vinyl-hunting trips to North America, wrote Kate Milestone in *Northern Soul.*

Record collecting has long been an ingrained part of DJ culture and remains important despite most DJs now choosing to perform using digital decks and MP3 files. Before the days of digital

ICONIC **COVERS**

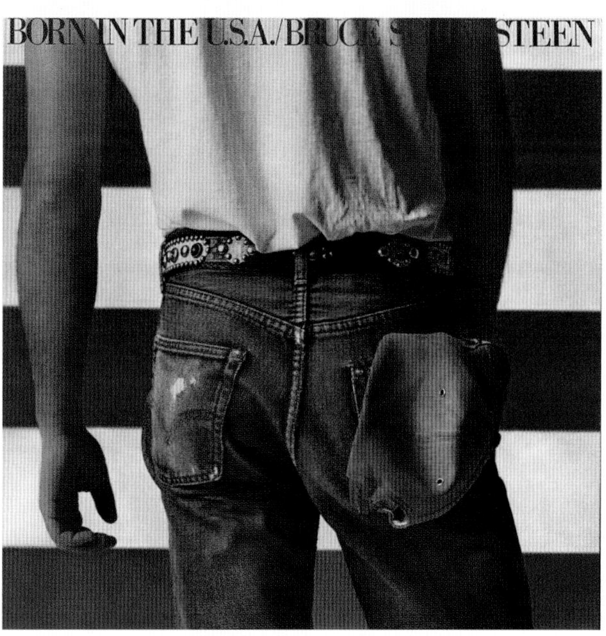

BORN IN THE U.S.A.

BRUCE SPRINGSTEEN

Springsteen (recently put in fine fettle after hitting the gym) is shot from behind by famed photographer Annie Leibovitz, and the focus is indeed his behind. The ball cap, jeans, and white T-shirt signaled identification with the workingman; and the stripes from the American flag added nationalism to the presentation, underscored by the record's titling. *–M.P.*

REMARKABLE **RECORD STORES**

GEORGE'S SONG SHOP • *JOHNSTOWN, PENNSYLVANIA*

Opened in 1932 by brothers Eugene and Bernie George, this store (sixty miles east of Pittsburgh) holds the record as being the oldest record shop in the United States. Eugene's son, John, runs the shop today. George's boasts of having over 1 million records and CDs in stock, inspiring its motto, "If we don't have it, nobody does!" The current location is spread over five floors, and you'll find records piled high in the stairwells. –*G.G.*

music, most people who turned to DJing did so because they already had an insatiable record collecting habit. What better way to showcase the gems in your growing collection than to play them to people in public?

To satisfy the demands of dance floors, new and little-known records are always needed. Having records that your rivals and contemporaries don't have—whether you're a northern soul DJ or you play cutting-edge dance music—is just as big a badge of honor for DJs as demonstrating an ability to entertain a dance floor. It's certainly more important than being able to seamlessly mix two records together, as the rise of the "selector"—DJs renowned for finding, selecting, and showcasing rare and forgotten records—over the last decade has shown.

Because of this, there are plenty of DJs around the world with impressive record collections. Not all are huge—some prefer to keep a set number of records or regularly refresh their collection by selling portions before buying other records to put in their place—but they're all cherished, are lovingly curated, and provide the tools of their chosen trade.

The size of DJs' collections can also be artificially inflated by "doubles"—second copies of a record bought either as a backup or to aid with performance. During the early stages of the hip-hop scene in New York during the 1970s, leading DJs would entertain dancers by mixing between two copies of the same record. This effectively allowed them to extend key instrumental passages of records—known as the "breaks"—to create their own versions "on the fly." Many club DJs of the 1980s and 1990s used the same techniques, with the aid of "doubles" of key tracks, to perform live remixes during their sets.

This is one reason why some veteran DJs end up with gigantic collections, some of which end up being donated to record libraries (a few exist around the world, including one at the British Library in London, which boasts well over 1 million discs). New York–based DJ and music producer François Kevorkian reportedly regularly donates records to Bob George's ARChive, while hip-hop pioneer Afrika Bambaataa's 43,000-strong collection is now stored and managed by Cornell University.

Hip-hop music's love affair with records has traditionally been almost total. Aside from needing "doubles" for DJing performances, those DJs who are also beat makers and music producers also swell their collections by picking up records to sample in their tracks. A sample is a short musical loop—a snatch of groove, a portion of a lead vocal, or an instrumental solo—that can be used to help build a new beat or backing track. Some classic hip-hop tracks contain dozens of samples, each lifted from a different record. Because of this, hip-hop DJs and producers devote tons of time to finding records containing possible samples, increasing the size of their collections in the process.

DJs, music producers, and the "extreme collectors" mentioned earlier are naturally among the most visible and high-profile vinyl addicts in the world; but in truth, many avid collectors are hobbyists who don't get hung up about the number of albums they own. These people care about vinyl and the environment in which they store and listen to records but have no "completist" aims.

For proof, check out photographer Eilon Paz's Dust & Grooves website (dustandgrooves.com), which features interviews with record collectors scattered across the globe, accompanied by pictures of them with their collections. While some are DJs

← Many avid collectors don't get hung up on the number of albums they own. They care about vinyl and the environment in which they store and listen to records but have no "completist" aims.

or high-profile hoarders, others are just enthusiasts who use collecting and keeping records as a release from the daily stresses of twenty-first-century life. The reasons cited by interviewees for becoming collectors, and what their collection means to them, are as varied as they are life affirming.

Logan Melissa, for example, is obsessed by record covers and sleeve artwork. Her obsession is such that she runs a popular Instagram account, Height Five Seven, in which she posts staged re-creations of some of her favorite album covers.

"I sometimes get people asking me if I actually listen to the records I'm re-creating—of course I do," Melissa is quoted as telling Paz. "I love these records! I wouldn't be doing this if I wasn't passionate about music. I always write something that shows I care about the album. The producer, the musicians, the year it came out, what else came out around the same time . . . I want it to be clear that this isn't just some art project I do; it's a way of honoring the music I love."

THE PRACTICALITIES OF RECORD COLLECTING

We've looked into the psychology of record collecting and ascertained that there's never been a better time to be a collector. But what about the practical aspects of the hobby? Over the course of the remainder of this chapter, we're going to offer up some smart advice on building up a collection, storing and managing it, and creating the right environment to get the most out of it.

Since record shops are discussed at length elsewhere in this book, we'll start by outlining other ways to add LPs to your collection. It's never been easier to find and buy vinyl records. You can find them for sale in all manner of places—think yard sales, vintage stores, and dedicated record dealers who email out lists of available items to keen collectors—but the most popular places to find and trade records now are online marketplaces.

The biggest players in the game, eBay and Amazon Marketplace, are naturally well worth a look (the latter in particular, as new releases are often listed as well as previously owned secondhand ones); but the biggest player is Discogs (discogs.com), a dedicated music marketplace.

Discogs started life as an online music database run by enthusiastic record collectors—a tool for vinyl addicts and researchers that listed physical music products and key details about them. As of 2022, the database now lists more than 50 million different items, according to Brian Coney and *DJ* magazine—a huge number of which can be bought and sold through the site's popular marketplace. Many collectors use this to buy and sell records, from people looking to downsize or give up their

ICONIC **COVERS**

REIGN IN BLOOD

SLAYER

Even the band thought the painting provided by *Village Voice* and *New York Times* illustrator Larry Carroll was too disturbing, with Kerry King calling him "a warped, demented freak." But there's no question this image raised the game on the amateurish Satanic art on the front of heavy metal albums previous. *—M.P.*

A BEGINNER'S GUIDE TO RECORD GRADING

When it comes to buying and selling records, most retailers aimed at collectors (including the Discogs marketplace and many secondhand stores) use the same standard record grading system, known as the Goldmine Grading Guide. Both the "media" (the record itself) and the sleeve are given grades, which range from "poor" (crackly or warped records, badly damaged sleeves) to "near mint" and "mint" (practically perfect and often sealed or unplayed). The value, and therefore the selling price, of a release is calculated using these gradings. For further information, check the Goldmine Grading Guide online (goldminemag.com/collector-resources/record-grading-101).

ABBREVIATIONS

M	MINT
NM	NEAR MINT (SOMETIMES M-)
VG+	VERY GOOD PLUS (SOMETIMES E FOR "EXCELLENT")
VG	VERY GOOD
G+	GOOD PLUS (SOMETIMES VG-)
G	GOOD
F	FAIR
P	POOR

← Luckily the hobby has a standard scale for determining the condition—and value—of records.

prized collections, to the owners of physical record stores and dealers who specialize in rare records.

The website tends not to trumpet how many records are bought and sold via its marketplace, but it does frequently run articles on the most expensive items bought from sellers on the platform. The current record for the highest price ever paid on the site is over $41,000, for a rare and exceedingly limited record called *Choose Your Weapon* by British DJ Scaramanga Silk.

That's the sort of price you'd expect to pay in an auction of rare music memorabilia at somewhere like Sotheby's or Christie's, though naturally records have sold for far more at one of those events. In 2015 the first copy of The Beatles' "White Album" ever manufactured fetched an astonishing $790,000 at Julien's in Beverly Hills!

Mercifully most records bought and sold on Discogs are nowhere near as expensive. The beauty of Discogs is that, with a few exceptions, you can pretty much find anything for sale—from long-forgotten "hidden gems" and rare "private press" albums (LPs never commercially released and originally either given away for free or sold by musicians directly to fans) to million-sellers and the newest vinyl releases.

How much you pay for a release varies massively, of course, with the basics of supply and demand—meaning sought-after or scarce releases sometimes change hands for eye-watering sums. Even limited-edition or in-demand new releases can end up selling for inflated amounts, though, with some "flippers" deliberately snapping up records on other stores before relisting them for sale at higher prices on Discogs.

While this can be infuriating for collectors, there are far more records listed for sale on Discogs at affordable or inexpensive prices. As ever, it depends on what you're looking for and the condition that the record and sleeve are in. For example, you could easily find a crackly old copy of a platinum-selling album from the 1980s for a few dollars; but a pristine "near mint" copy—a grading suggesting that it has been barely played and stored impeccably—would cost you far more (see "A Beginner's Guide to Record Grading").

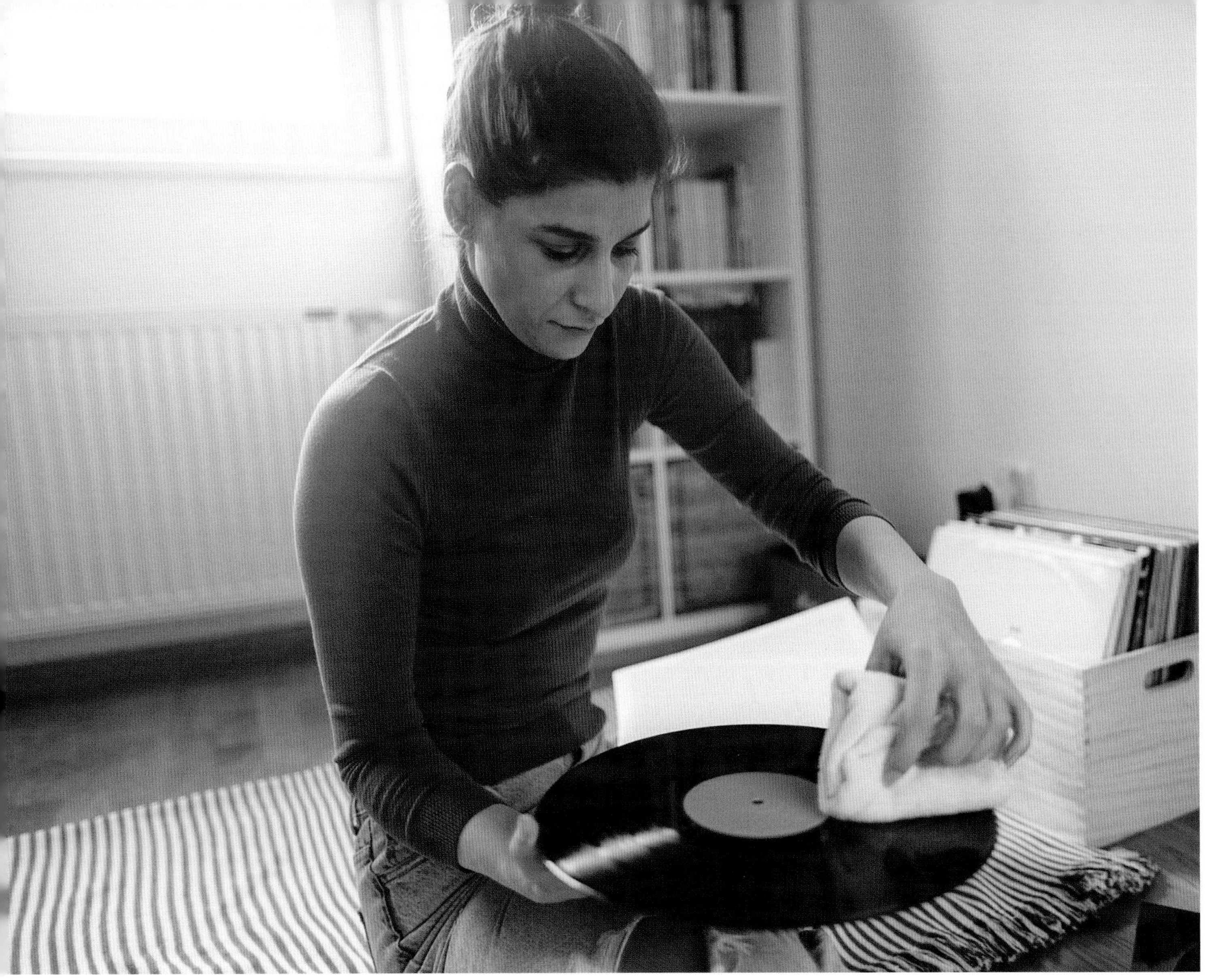

↑ Before and after each play, use the "dry cleaning" method. With a carbon fiber brush or microfiber cloth, wipe with the grooves in a circular motion, from the center outward.

TAKE CARE

The record grading system, where albums kept in great condition are naturally considered to be of higher value, offers a timely reminder that taking care of your record collection is imperative. As a physical medium that replicates sound through contact between two objects—the stylus attached to the tonearm of your turntable and the surface of the disc—vinyl records change over time. The grooves become worn down and, without regular cleaning, a haven for dust and dirt. Not only will your records be less valuable in this state, but more importantly, they will also

LEGENDARY **LABELS**

SUB POP

Almost synonymous with Seattle's grunge rock sound in the late 1980s and early 1990s, Sub Pop was a cornerstone of the movement with early releases by Nirvana, Soundgarden, and Mudhoney. Cofounded by Jonathan Poneman and Bruce Pavitt, it quickly built a brand not just with its recognizable black-and-white logo and cover graphics but also by issuing batches of collectible limited-edition singles and launching a Sub Pop Singles Club with monthly singles for subscribers. Although Sub Pop entered a partnership with Warner Brothers that ended its totally independent status in the mid-1990s, it branched into other forms of adventurous, sometimes non-punk or non-grunge alternative rock with acts like Low, Jeremy Enigk, Eric Matthews, and Sleater-Kinney. A split resulted in Pavitt leaving the label in the mid-1990s and, in the view of some longtime followers, diluting its fiercely maverick spirit. *–R.U.*

ICONIC **COVERS**

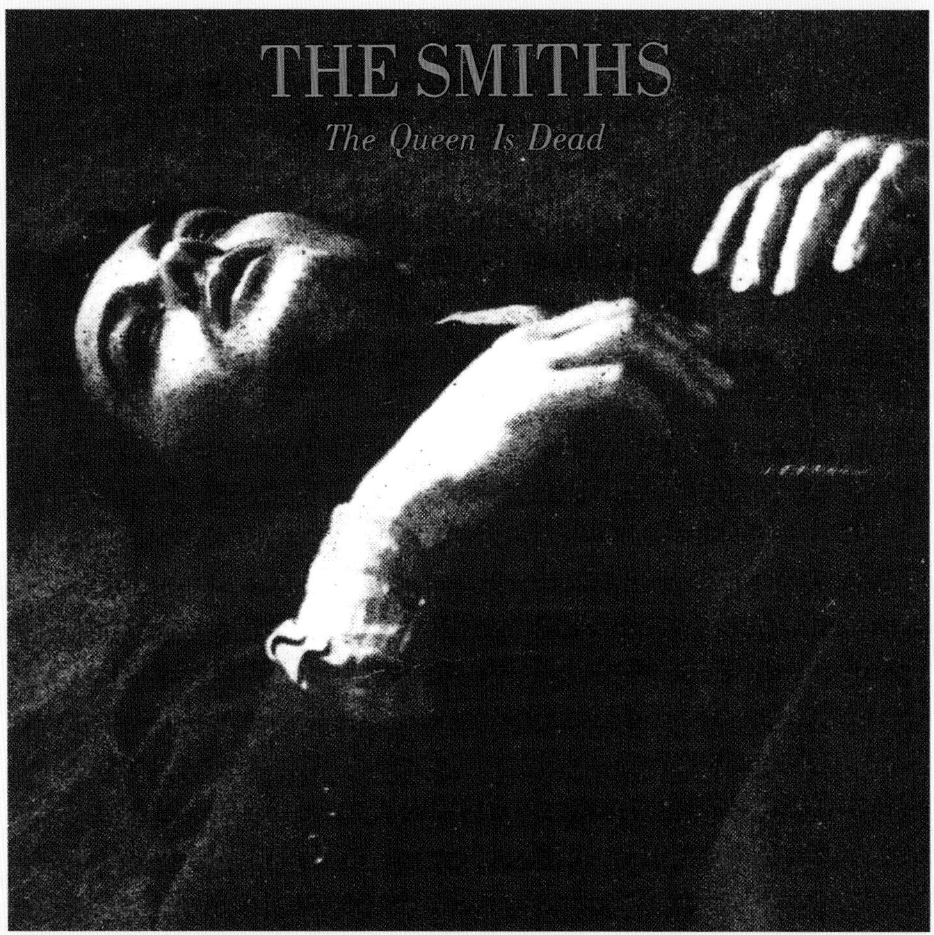

THE QUEEN IS DEAD • THE SMITHS

A dramatic still of actor Alain Delon from the French film *L'Insoumis*. The almost-oppressive emerald green suggests Britain and its rainy weather, while the splash of pink suggests Sex Pistols. Maybe it ain't much to look at on its own, but grouped with the band's other album covers, a distinct gloomy Manchester narrative emerges. *–M.P.*

sound far worse, with pops and crackles potentially ruining the listening experience.

Fortunately it is possible to slow down the progress of degradation, not only to the surface of the record but also to the sleeve that it comes with. Getting a good-quality stylus helps (higher-grade diamond stylus tips are not as blunt), as does setting the tonearm's counterweight so that the needle doesn't dig into the surface of the record during playback.

Handling records carefully, ideally avoiding contact from your fingertips on the LP's playing area, is also important. But the number-one thing you can do to keep your vinyl in tip-top condition is to clean them regularly. There are several ways of doing this, and experts suggest that combining these methods is the best way of keeping your vinyl in good shape.

For regular cleaning, ideally before and after each play, use so-called "dry cleaning." This is when you use a carbon fiber brush or microfiber cloth to wipe with the grooves in a circular motion, from the center outwards, taking care not to put your fingertips on the face of the platter. This will get rid of a fair bit of dust, but it won't remove caked-on dirt or dust that's gotten deep into the grooves. For that, you'll need to do a spot of "wet cleaning."

Many record shops sell bottles of record cleaning fluid. Spray a little of this onto the surface of the LP—a couple of sprays of fluid per side should do it—and then use your microfiber cloth or pad to clean and buff up the record. Once done, the record will look visibly cleaner and sound far better. If this doesn't do the trick, or if you're desperate for the best-quality cleaning solution, then our advice would be to invest in a record-cleaning system, sometimes known as record-cleaning machines.

There are quite a few different types of record-cleaning machines. At the cheapest end of the scale are manual cleaning systems where a record is clamped in place and then slowly moved through a bath of cleaning fluid which features in-built brushes. At the other end, you'll find automatic, motorized machines that either use a similar approach (with the addition of ultrasonic waves to help removed hard-to-shift dirt) or utilize a vacuum system to effectively suck dirt off the surface of the record. These get brilliant results but can be expensive. For example, a "spin-washer" vinyl bath will set you back between $75 and $150, while a top-end motorized machine could cost anything between $700 and $1,500. Fortunately there are many price points in between and multiple models to choose from, so do a little research before making your purchase.

The other thing you need to take care of is the record's packaging, known as the sleeve. First and foremost, always use "inner" sleeves. These offer a thin paper barrier between the surface of the record and the card outer sleeve and are proven to reduce the amount of dust that gets into the grooves during storage. In addition, it's also worth investing in plastic "outer sleeves," which help prevent wear and tear to the album's packaging during storage. Speaking of storage, it's important to put records away after use—leaving a record out on your turntable is a surefire way of getting it dusty and dirty very quickly!

SHOWING OFF YOUR COLLECTION

There are countless available record-storage solutions, but the absolute key to storing your records properly is to keep them upright. Piling them up on top of each other, as if stacking sheets of paper, is a sure way of damaging them. As you'd expect in this scenario, records toward the bottom of the pile will feel the weight of all those above and can become cracked or warped. Records stored upright, on a slant, can also potentially warp; so if you can, try and keep them as close to vertical as you can. Remember, too, to keep your records out of direct sunlight and away from heating sources such as radiators and fires.

What record storage you need will depend on how many albums you own and the space you have within your home to devote to the collection. If you live in a small apartment, you may only have space for an all-in-one turntable stand and shelving unit, a sole shelf, or a small turntable display table and a couple of wooden crates to store your LPs. If you have a few hundred or a couple thousand records, then you'll need to find a shelving unit or two in which to store your prized collection.

Vinyl-specific shelving units need not be too expensive. The world's most popular shelving for storing records, at least anecdotally, comes from flat-pack furniture retailer IKEA. Their Kallax shelving units, and the now-discontinued Expedit range, are near perfect for storing records and come in various size configurations. Plenty of other manufacturers offer similar shelving units, some of which are customizable or can be made to your specifications—so take a good look online before making your decision.

The other alternative, of course, is to splash out on custom-built furniture and, if you have the space in your home, a dedicated listening room to house your treasured collection. While this is impractical for many people, having a space to indulge your hobby and immerse yourself in music is the ultimate for any collector.

The joy of having your own listening room is that you can configure it however you wish. It can be created from scratch with bespoke record shelves and a hi-fi storage unit (or extended "deck table" if you're a DJ and own two turntables and a mixer) or put together using easily available, mass-manufactured

→ The joy of having your own listening room is that you can configure it however you wish. It can be created from scratch with bespoke record shelves and a hi-fi storage unit or put together using easily available, mass-manufactured units.

SPILLERS RECORDS EST 1894
DIM FFAIR ARFAU YNG NGHAERDYDD
NO ARMS FAIR IN CARDIFF
JOHN MOUSE
FREE LIVE MUSIC!
EUROS CHILDS
OPEN
OPENING HOURS:
MINTY'S GIGGUIDE TO CARDIFF
FREE MAP!
CARGO COLLECTIVE
PLEASE ASK INSIDE FOR MORE DETAILS!
NEW YEAR BARGAINS!
LOTS OF GREAT NEW YEAR DEALS HITTING THE RACKS
From QUEEN & U2, to RYAN ADAMS, KENDIRCK LAMAR & More!
COME IN TO FIND A BARGAIN!

REMARKABLE **RECORD STORES**

SPILLERS RECORDS

CARDIFF, WALES

Said to be the oldest record store in world, Spillers opened in 1894, named after its owner, Henry Spiller. It's a store that easily transitioned from wax cylinders to vinyl to CDs over the years, becoming such an institution that an international community rallied around when it was faced with the prospect of closure in 2010 (both Manic Street Preachers and Beyoncé came out in support). Located at Morgan Arcade at the time of writing, it's also known for its popular in-stores and friendly staff. *–G.G.*

storage units. If you enjoy reading about music, you might want to add a small bookcase to house biographies of bands and deluxe books on record-collecting culture. You might also dedicate a corner of the room to your record-cleaning machine and accessories. As it's your listening room, you can add your own decorative touches, too, such as displays of other music memorabilia, framed posters, or displays of your favorite album sleeves (several companies sell frames that LP covers neatly slip inside).

More importantly, you can also place the speakers to make the best use of the space. As a rule, you'll get the best-quality sound if you put speakers on stands, keep them away from walls and other bulky objects with hard surfaces, and space them out. The latter aspect naturally allows better stereo reproduction but also helps fill the room with sound. Really dedicated audiophiles may also fit the walls and ceilings of their listening rooms with soundproof material to enhance the acoustics, but this is an expensive and time-consuming step that makes a difference only if you have the highest-quality hi-fi components and equipment. For 99 percent of record collectors, it's unnecessary.

Most people buy a single pair of speakers, but many amplifiers have connectors for a second pair, with the option of either switching between the two or using all four speakers at the same time. While this wouldn't provide true cinema-style "surround sound" (that requires digital music mastered for a system such as Dolby Atmos and a specialist amplifier), it's as close as you'll get with vinyl records.

Ideally the sofa or armchairs you use when listening to records should be equidistant between the speakers. While this isn't always possible, you can change the angle of your speakers and the direction they point in quite easily. When setting up your listening space, play around with positioning until you're happy with what you hear. Once you are, you can sit back, throw an album on, and listen, surrounded by the collection you've so lovingly built and stored. For a keen record collector, there's no better feeling. ◊

RESOURCES

CHAPTER 2

musicdirect.com/equipment/book/ortofon-a-century-of-accuracy-in-sound-100th-anniversary-book/

barnesandnoble.com/w/revolution-gideon-schwartz/1141367898

thevinylfactory.com/news/pro-ject-launches-all-in-one-colourful-audio-system/

www.whathifi.com/features/12-weird-and-wonderful-turntable-designs

stuff.tv/features/7-craziest-turntables-you-can-buy-today/

gearpatrol.com/tech/audio/g39075225/best-turntables-under-500/

nytimes.com/wirecutter/reviews/best-turntable/

devotedtovinyl.com/whats-the-best-all-in-one-record-player-to-buy/

techradar.com/news/best-turntables

whathifi.com/us/best-buys/hi-fi/best-turntables

rollingstone.com/product-recommendations/electronicsbest-record-players-budget-affordable-turntables-780295/

audioreputation.com/all-in-one-stereo-systems-with-turntables/

whathifi.com/features/the-trouble-with-all-in-one-turntables-and-what-to-buy-instead

TURNTABLE LAB SYSTEM

turntablelab.com/products/audio-technica-at-lp60xusb-edifier-r1280db-turntable-package-ttl-setup?variant=32880816455770¤cy=USD&utm_medium=product_sync&utm_source=google&utm_content=sag_organic&utm_campaign=sag_organic&gclid=Cj0KCQiAofieBhDXARIsAHTTldq_tMUdikBKF14EIDk62ZvZZm3w0-acb_9_sJn8fSp1Jgkx-zZudkEaAmhvEALw_wcB

CROSLEY ALL IN ONE

amazon.com/dp/B074CRKQRK?tag=soundjunky-20

1 BY ONE ALL IN ONE

amazon.com/ONE-Fidelity-Turntable-Bluetooth-Cartridge/dp/B0B38VFQ4C/ref=pd_lpo_1?pd_rd_w=4CNWx&content-id=amzn1.sym.196193c7-f80f-4550-90d9-c8be3a442748&pf_rd_p=196193c7-f80f-4550-90d9-c8be3a442748&pf_rd_r=QYXM1ZY9RYWADSCZAPAG&pd_rd_wg=PZrnK&pd_rd_r=0dba80d3-d6fb-45ba-9a46-7b3af54019c6&pd_rd_i=B0B38VFQ4C&psc=1

SEPARATES

amazon.com/Bluetooth-Turntable-Bookshelf-Speakers-Cartridge/dp/B07H8VG9BB/ref=pd_lpo_3?pd_rd_w=4CNWx&content-id=amzn1.sym.196193c7-f80f-4550-90d9-c8be3a442748&pf_rd_p=196193c7-f80f-4550-90d9-c8be3a442748&pf_rd_r=QYXM1ZY9RYWADSCZAPAG&pd_rd_wg=PZrnK&pd_rd_r=0dba80d3-d6fb-45ba-9a46-7b3af54019c6&pd_rd_i=B07H8VG9BB&psc=1

PRO-JECT SONOS PACKAGE

turntablelab.com/products/pro-ject-t1-sb-phono-sonos-five-turntable-package-ttl-setup?variant=32424556167258¤cy=USD&utm_medium=product_sync&utm_source=google&utm_content=sag_organic&utm_campaign=sag_organic&gclid=Cj0KCQiAofieBhDXARIsAHTTldqBB-zeRo3bZGcdnVwXDNNZhjjMfcGMsrJGOT8Zv6TkiKQ5Vt5B-rMaAnngEALw_wcB

WRENSILVA COMPACT

wrensilva.com/collections/stereo-consoles/products/loft-modern-stereo-console?&utm_medium=cpc&utm_source=google&utm_campaign=Google%20

WRENSILVA ALL IN ONE

wrensilva.com/products/standard-one-hifi-audio-system?&utm_medium=cpc&utm_source=google&utm_campaign=Google%20Shopping&gclid=Cj0KCQiAofieBhDXARIsAHTTldrSxQYXfbPUxoaEGzZJqbMVF93iLH4hQM6HlGZ10nb-COl5J06metYaAueaEALw_wcB

WRENSILVA M1

wrensilva.com/products/wrensilva-m1-modern-hifi-stereo-console?&utm_medium=cpc&utm_source=google&utm_campaign=Google%20Shopping&gclid=Cj0KCQiAofieBhDXARIsAHTTldq0aF8Q6GTu96OKwjjINxlizsnDCaQoHSWtLGRRoCLYfpJMBGLgyAcaAtyJEALw_wcB

LX X | LA BOITE CONCEPT

laboiteconcept.com/en/products/lxx/

CLASS-D AMPLIFIER

wikipedia.org/wiki/Class-D_amplifier

IMAGE CREDITS

B = bottom, I = inset, L = left, M = main, R = right, T = top

Alamy Stock Photos: 4, Malcolm Fairman; 9B, Bygone Collection; 12, Robert Landau; 18, Richard Levine; 21, Retro AdArchives; 26, Cathyrose Melloan; 27, Nick Moore; 33, Shawshots; 35T, Vinyls; 37, Vinyls; 50i, CBW; 58–59, Birgit Reitz-Hofmann; 61, cuong nguyen; 62, pxl.store; 63, Pavel Chernobrivets; 64, Konstantin Gushcha; 66, lowepix; 67, Marcin Kosciolek; 73, John Muggenborg; 74, Niday Picture Library; 76, Elizabeth Leyden; 77, H. Armstrong Roberts; 82B, Valeriy Novikov; 87, 4k-Clips; 88, ICP; 99L, ZUMA; 104B, Records; 105, Records; 112, Kay Roxby; 116, David Lichtneker; 117, CBW; 119T, Jurga Kalinauskaite; 120, Colin Underhill; 123, Elly Godfroy; 125, Felix Choo; 130T, Southern Stock Photo; 132T, TCD/Prod.DB; 139, Iconographic Archive; 143, Frank Nowikowski;144–145, Matthew Chattle; 146B, WENN; 152, UrbanImages; 155, Hufton+Crow-VIEW; 156, Elly Godfroy; 157B, CI2; 161, Adam Melnyk; 163, Adrian Weston; 168, WENN; 174, Przemyslaw Klos. **Associated Press:** 147, John Stillwell; 149, Mark Humphrey; 167, Carolyn Bauman. **Bridgeman Images:** 14, Milou Steiner/Photopress Archiv/Keystone; 16–17, Underwood Archives/UIG; 71, Everett Collection; 101L, Keystone; 104T, Bridgeman Images; 132B, © Classic Picture Library; 136T, SuperStock. **Creative Commons:** 80, Thegreenj/CC BY-SA 3.0; 84, Sakurambo-commonswiki, CC BY-SA 2.5. **Getty Images:** 2, Hulton Deutsch/Corbis Historical; 7, Marco Vacca/Photodisc; 8BR, Science & Society Picture Library; 10, ullstein bild; 11B, Daily Herald Archive; 22, Archive Photos; 24–25, FPG; 28, Kim Vintage Stock; 38M, Bettmann; 42M, Evening Standard/Hulton Archive; 47, San Francisco Chronicle/Hearst Newspapers; 49, Lynn Goldsmith; 50M, Paul Natkin; 53, SOPA Images/LightRocket; 54, San Francisco Chronicle/Hearst Newspapers; 57,Susumu Yoshioka/DigitalVision; 94, John Pratt/Hulton Archive; 97, Kamil Krzaczynski/AFP; 98M, Michael Putland/Hulton Archive; 99R, © Ted Streshinsky/Corbis; 103R, Evening Standard/Hulton Archive; 106, Mirrorpix; 110, Chris Morphet/Hulton Archive; 118, Estate of Keith Morris/Redferns; 119B, Picture Alliance; 127, Michael Ochs Archives; 128, William P. Gottlieb/Redferns; 135, Metallica; 136N, Tom Hill/WireImage; 140, Mirrorpix; 146T, Boston Globe; 150, Michael Ochs Archives; 164, The Washington Post; 165, The Washington Post; 172, Sam Mellish/In Pictures; 181, Markus Moellenberg/Corbis. **Rusty Glessner (pabucketlist.com):** 170. **Library of Congress:** 91, William P. Gottlieb (LC-GLB23-0813 DLC); 96, William P. Gottlieb (LC-GLB13- 0611). **MPTV:** 109M, © Ed Thrasher. **National Park Service:** 8–9T. **Dennis Pernu:** 120, 130B, 133. **Shutterstock:** 11T, Light and Vision; 65TL, rossiaa33; 68, rossiaa33; 71, rossiaa33; 82T, Igor Gallo Kalassa; 113, FocusFantastic; 158, James Kirkikis; 166, PhakornS; 176, Sensay; 182, John Selway; 184, Sensay. **Waterloo Records:** 70.

AUTHOR BIOGRAPHIES

Matt Anniss is an author, journalist, speaker, DJ, and content creator with over twenty years' experience. Anniss rose to prominence following the publication of his critically acclaimed exploration of bleep techno and the foundations of the "U.K. bass" sound, *Join the Future: Bleep Techno and the Birth of British Bass Music* (2019). He is also the coauthor of the bestselling *The Vinyl Manual,* and his work has appeared in *International DJ Magazine* (*IDJ*), *DJ* magazine, *Mixmag*, and elsewhere.

Gillian G. Gaar has written for numerous publications, including *Mojo*, *Rolling Stone*, and *Goldmine*. Her other books include *She's a Rebel: The History of Women in Rock & Roll*; *Entertain Us: The Rise of Nirvana*; *Return of the King: Elvis Presley's Great Comeback*; *The Doors: The Complete Illustrated History*; *Elton John at 75*; and *Bruce Springsteen at 75*. She lives in Seattle.

Ken Micallef is a New York–based freelance journalist, contributing to *Stereophile* magazine, AnalogPlanet.com, and *Downbeat*. Ken spends his spare time buying and selling vacuum tubes and growing his already-massive collection of jazz records, with a focus on the recordings of Eddie Lockjaw Davis and Trini Lopez. When in New York, Ken can be found most weekends at the Jazz Record Center.

Working out of Toronto, Canada, **Martin Popoff** (martinpopoff.com) has penned more than 100 books on hard rock, heavy metal, classic rock, and record collecting, including *Rush: The Illustrated History*, *Bowie at 75, Pink Floyd and The Dark Side of the Moon,* and *The Who and Quadrophenia*. In addition, he has appeared in *Revolver*, *Guitar World*, *Goldmine*, *Record Collector*, bravewords.com, lollipop.com, and hardradio.com. Martin also worked on the award-winning documentaries *Rush: Beyond the Lighted Stage* and *ZZ Top: That Little Ol' Band from Texas* for Banger Films.

Richie Unterberger is the author of numerous rock history books, including *The Unreleased Beatles: Music and Film*, which won a 2007 Association for Recorded Sound Collections Award for Excellence in Historical Recorded Sound Research in the "Best Discography" division of the "Best Research in Recorded Rock Music" category. His other books include *Fleetwood Mac: The Ultimate Illustrated History* and *Bob Marley and the Wailers: The Ultimate Illustrated History*. He is a frequent contributor to *MOJO* and *Record Collector*, and he teaches courses on rock music history at the College of Marin, the University of San Francisco, and City College of San Francisco.

INDEX

Quarto.com

© 2023 Quarto Publishing Group USA Inc.

First Published in 2023 by Motorbooks, an imprint of The Quarto Group,
100 Cummings Center, Suite 265-D, Beverly, MA 01915, USA.
T (978) 282-9590 F (978) 283-2742

All rights reserved. No part of this book may be reproduced in any form without written permission of the copyright owners. All images in this book have been reproduced with the knowledge and prior consent of the artists concerned, and no responsibility is accepted by producer, publisher, or printer for any infringement of copyright or otherwise, arising from the contents of this publication. Every effort has been made to ensure that credits accurately comply with information supplied. We apologize for any inaccuracies that may have occurred and will resolve inaccurate or missing information in a subsequent reprinting of the book.

Motorbooks titles are also available at discount for retail, wholesale, promotional, and bulk purchase. For details, contact the Special Sales Manager by email at specialsales@quarto.com or by mail at The Quarto Group, Attn: Special Sales Manager, 100 Cummings Center, Suite 265-D, Beverly, MA 01915, USA.

27 26 25 24 23   2 3 4 5

ISBN: 978-0-7603-8331-5

Digital edition published in 2022
eISBN: 978-0-7603-8332-2

Library of Congress Cataloging-in-Publication Data

Names: Anniss, Matt, author. | Gaar, Gillian G., 1959- author. | Micallef, Ken, author. | Popoff, Martin, 1963- author. | Unterberger, Richie, 1962- author.
Title: In the groove : the vinyl record and turntable revolution / Matt Anniss, Gillian G. Gaar, Ken Micallef, Martin Popoff & Richie Unterberger.
Description: Beverly : Motorbooks, 2023. | Includes bibliographical references and index. | Summary: "Coinciding with the 75th anniversary of the first commercial LP, In the Groove is an authoritative and visual celebration of the history and culture of vinyl record collecting and turntables"— Provided by publisher.
Identifiers: LCCN 2023015658 | ISBN 9780760383315 (hardcover) | ISBN 9780760383322 (ebook)
Subjects: LCSH: Sound recordings--Collectors and collecting. | Phonograph turntables—Collectors and collecting. | Sound recordings—History. | Sound recording industry—History.
Classification: LCC ML1055 .I53 2023 | DDC 780.26/6—dc23/eng/20230406
LC record available at https://lccn.loc.gov/2023015658

Design and Page Layout: The Sly Studio | theslystudio.com
Cover Illustration: Shutterstock
Cover Image: Popperfoto/Getty Images
Endpaper: Shutterstock

Printed in China